Kicking Apps
and
Making Names

Want more personal help Kicking Apps? Need guidance about how to Make your Name?

Platt and Chiofalo are available to help.

Contact us today:

www.kickingapps.org

kickingappsmakingnames@gmail.com

386-405-2128

<u>Individual Assistance</u>

Comprehensive College Consulting · Essay review

Resume development · Project design · Mentorship

<u>Large Group programs available as well</u>

One day college application workshops · Week long bootcamps

Staff professional development · Motivational speaking

Table of Contents

Chapter 1:

Kicking Apps and Making Names

1.1 How can you kick apps and make a name for yourself?

For students and families today, navigating the high-stakes college admissions landscape can seem daunting, frustrating, and at times even completely overwhelming. This guide is designed to help demystify this process for both you and your family, and help make the admissions process a successful and productive growth experience. But, for this to happen you will have to start planning and working hard early in high school, not just during senior year. When this process is done effectively, you will come alive on the screen and your application will convince the admissions counselors that you will make an invaluable contribution to their university. In simple terms, the application shows the college who you are and how smart you are. What you have done and the level at which you have done it displays to admissions counselors the impact you will make at their university.

Kicking apps means that you kick ass during this process, you own it, you put your best foot forward and you achieve what you are hoping for. To be clear, you can't kick apps overnight; it will take time and deliberate planning. This guide is designed to help you do just that. Whether you are a senior getting serious about the process just in time or an underclassman with long term goals who is ready to establish plans to achieve them now, this guide is for you.

The first half of the guide focuses on the long-term planning for college success, while the second half focuses primarily on the actual college application process that takes place during senior year. Though they are separated in this guide, these are not two independent events; they are, in fact, intimately connected with one another.

If you really want to kick apps, you will also need to make a name for yourself- and this guide will help you do exactly that. You need to have a story that is compelling, attractive to colleges and distinguishes you from your peers. You will become a student that a college will want on its campus. In the end, following the steps outlined in this guide will allow you to be kicking apps and making names.

1.2 What will your story be

So let's begin. There is no one right "story" for a student to embody. There is no one thing that will guarantee admission to the college of your dreams. Curing cancer or creating the next ubiquitous social networking technology before you graduate high school would, of course, help you immensely. But you don't have to be a child prodigy to earn admission to the university of your dreams. Success in the college application process can be broken down into 3 elements- the focal points of your approach to high school and the organizing ideas in this book.

1. **Earn high grades in rigorous classes**

2. **Achieve strong scores on standardized tests including: SAT®, ACT®, PSAT, SAT Subject tests, AP, IB, AICE**

3. **Develop a compelling story - the rest of everything you do beyond those grades and scores**

Now that you know the targets you can begin to think of ways to achieve them. Rule No. 1: Something is always better than nothing. Unless you are looking to play your Nietzsche card and become the nihilist on campus, you need to do something. You need to be someone. That is essentially what you will achieve by focusing on those three elements in your approach. So a reasonable beginning question is, How high do you want to shoot? This process looks very different if your end goal is a two-year associate degree compared to admission to Stanford. Start by thinking about some goals- personal, academic, athletic and others. You may want to fill in this chart with pencil as these goals will likely change as you grow.

High School Goals

Long Term Goals / Life Goals	
1	
2	
3	
Freshman Year	
1	
2	
Sophomore Year	
1	
2	

Junior Year	
1	
2	
Senior Year	
1	
2	

Revisit these goals at least once a quarter, and don't hesitate modify them as you progress through high school. You will change during your years in high school and your goals should change to reflect that.

1.3 Be someone, Be unique, Oh hell just be yourself

Artificial collections of different activities, events and awards are just that: artificial. If you start high school with a purpose you can navigate it successfully to create your story. The key is to work continuously to figure out who you want to present yourself as to admissions counselors. This is not to say that this should be your sole focus throughout high school, but rather as you purposefully navigate through this process (instead of haphazardly racing through) you should discover your true self- the genuine "you" that you present for admission to college. If you are already starting senior year as you read this guide, then you should focus on weaving together existing elements in your resume and filling in any gaps.

1.4 What does it look like when you make a name for yourself?

Though your story should be uniquely yours, it often helps to see how some others took shape. Making a name for yourself is key, and your individual spin is most important. Below you can find two successful students' stories.

Case Study of AN

When we had our first conversation with AN, during the spring of his sophomore year, he wanted to go to Princeton to study Biology and play Division I basketball, but as we began our work together his interests shifted organically. A mission trip to an impoverished area in El Salvador was followed by an influential year in an elective class, AP Environmental Science, which he took initially just for a GPA bump. While his IB education track continued toward Biology and Princeton, he joined the school's Envirothon team which he led to the state competition.

Princeton changed to Duke and basketball fell off the radar only to be replaced by volleyball (which he excelled in but never planned to pursue in college). This change left more time for him to venture into his environmental interests and he completed his senior research project and IB extended essay on eutrophication, which tied together the issues in Central America with those in his home state of Florida. Then, inspired by an elected leadership role in the school environmental club, he went out on his own to make a change on his school campus. He lobbied for, fundraised for, planned and eventually orchestrated the installation of an electric car charger in the student parking lot at his high school. Even after his early acceptance to Duke the fall of his senior year, he led his Envirothon team to fourth place in the state and became even more invested in his environmental pursuits.

AN's story is not a loose collection of activities; it is the manifestation of his pursuit of his interests and developing a story around a central idea. Again, there is no one right path to follow, no one story that is better than others, but a compelling story is hard for any school to ignore.

Case Study of BG

BG and her parents first contacted us at the start of her sophomore year. She had lofty aspirations and a desire to attend a selective school like Princeton. BG spent a lot of time playing sports and devoting herself to school but hadn't really found her direction or passion during the first few years of high school. Then, through the course of our preliminary discussions her interest in feminism surfaced. More specifically, she mentioned "selfie culture" and the impact she had seen it have on her own friends. That provided us with a starting point.

Early on, she identified giving women a voice as her main objective, which prompted her to begin a debate club at her school and teach students how to find their voice. The debate club flourished, but she felt like it didn't do enough to resolve the core problem, so BG began to think of ways to take her story further. With the desire to make a positive impact on the girls in her community, BG came up with the idea to create a mentoring program for middle school girls making the challenging transition to high school. So she created the Ophelia Project. For one day, young girls would meet with high school mentors and have frank discussions to help propel them to make strong, confident choices as they moved into high school. The girls' parents would also learn about relevant issues from a panel of local experts. For two years the Ophelia Project helped middle school girls in the community become self aware young women. BG took it a step further by joining a leadership program at the state level and advancing her agenda by raising awareness with state legislators. By the time she was ready to apply to college, she had realized that a smaller environment would allow her to benefit from similar mentorship so she applied and earned admission to both Tufts and Middlebury. Ultimately, she chose to attend Tufts.

So what are you interested in? Thinking about this in an organized fashion can help you to begin to decide what your own story will be.

Interest Inventory

What interests you?
What excites you?
What angers you?
What challenges you?
What would you change in the world?

1. Concluding Thoughts

As you progress through high school, it is easy to lose sight of the forest as you focus on all the trees. The tests, the activities, and the day-to-day challenges can easily distract you from the big picture of your four years. It is important, then, to begin with the end in mind. As you start to think about where you want to go to college, you will realize what you need to create for yourself while in high school. Remember that success in high school means gaining admission to the colleges of your choice. That doesn't happen on its own. It comes from making intentional decisions and purposefully planning your path.

1. Action Items

- ❏ Establish short-term and long-term goals
- ❏ Think about what interests you
- ❏ Start to develop a plan of attack - how you will approach whatever time is left in high school
- ❏ Start to think about what your story will be
- ❏ Begin to develop some ideas about college

Part 1:

Developing your story

Chapter 2:

Plan your time during high school

2.1 How to Organize your time

Organizing your time in high school is critically important. Far too often we work with students and families who get to senior year and application time only to utter the phrase "I never knew that I should have _____." To avoid this scenario it is imperative to begin with the end in mind. If you are purposeful in the way you approach each year then the outcome in college admissions should be favorable. Part of this advance scheduling should help to alleviate some of the stress, that comes during the later years of high school, by helping you to knock off items you will need in later years early on in the process.

2.2 Year-by-year Schedule

We have included a year by year schedule of events to help you make your name. This is the part where you will work to truly develop your story. If you are starting to use this workbook at any time after freshman year, be sure that you go back and revisit the items in the earlier years on this list to avoid potential holes in your story. For each year, we have targeted the different aspects that will help to bring together the full picture of who you are. We have included tables within each year for use as checklists to monitor the completion of different activities and provide you with a rough timetable to assist in scheduling. Space is provided for you to fill in other items that you complete each month and to write notes along the way. Active use of these organizers will not only ensure that you stay on track, but also that you record elements that you will later use for creating your resume among other things. Each year is divided into three parts: fall semester, spring semester and summer.

2.3 Freshman year

This is the year that can often be written off and lost as an adjustment period. That is a mistake. Freshman year is an opportunity to begin to separate yourself from your peers and start to figure out your interests and talents, both in and out of school. In addition remember that you will only get busier and the stakes will only get higher as you progress through high school. This is the year to take some risks and make a name for yourself. If you have the opportunity to take Advanced Placement® (AP) classes this year, your ensuing test scores can also comprise an important part of your college application. Remember if you are taking AP tests then you may have the possibility of taking SAT 2 Subject tests as well.

Fall Semester		
Month	Activity	Complete
Aug.	Get yourself a good paper calendar. Put in major deadlines (marking periods, midterms, tryouts, auditions, practices, games).	
	Set your goals for the first quarter.	
Sept.	Make a list of clubs or activities you would like to learn more about. Find out when they meet and attend the meetings.	
	Pick 1 activity that is completely outside of your comfort zone.	
	Find a charity or cause that interests you and volunteer.	
Oct.	Create a profile on Raise.me.	
	Review first quarter goals and set a semester goal to earn all A's	
Nov.	Vacations provide an opportunity to do something- take advantage of that.	
	Catch up on outstanding work and do some reading for fun.	

Dec.	Review PSAT 9 results if you have the opportunity to take it.	

Notes:	

Spring Semester

Month	Activity	Complete
Jan.	Consider your course selection for sophomore year.	
	Find summer programs and begin applications- apply to more than one in case you are rejected from some.	
Feb.	Finish your summer program applications.	
	Think about an independent project that you may be interested in starting in your community and beyond.	
March	If you haven't already met with your counselor, schedule an appointment to discuss your academic goals.	
April	Prepare for your AP exams.	

May	Take your first AP tests and remember that these count.	
	Consider taking SAT subject tests too if there is overlap.	
June	Finish the year strong academically.	

Notes:		

Summer after Freshman year		
Month	Activity	Complete
	Plan out a rigorous schedule to take for sophomore year considering junior and senior classes in the process.	
	Get some tutoring in advance for subjects that may be hard sophomore year or do preparation on you own.	
	Do your assigned summer reading but also do some just for fun.	
	Find something significant for your story.	

Notes:		

2.4 Sophomore year

This is the year when you will be making a lot of important decisions about your future academic track. The rigor of your courses should increase and any performance issues from freshman year should be ironed out or eliminated altogether. This is the year to fine tune your study skills or, for some, actually learn how to study. It is also the year for you to take your first real shot at standardized tests like the ACT® and SAT® if you are far enough along in math. The summer after this year will be a good opportunity to do something truly impactful. Remember by the end of your sophomore summer, you will have exhausted two-thirds of your opportunities to distinguish yourself during the summer.

Fall Semester		
Month	Activity	Complete
August	Write out your goals for the school year.	
	Start to conceptualize some sort of larger project for the year and beyond.	
	Decide on a social studies or science fair project for the year. Plan one and make it shine. If you don't complete one, then choose another academic competition to participate in.	

Sept.	Create a profile on the coalition application. Visit **www.coalitionforcollegeaccess.org** to begin.	
	Prep for the PSAT if you plan to take it	
	Start to determine your tutoring needs for school subjects.	
Oct.	Solidify your first quarter grades to get all A's.	
	Take the PSAT 10 and give your best effort. If you have testing concerns you may want to do some prep for this test.	
Nov.	Solidify semester grades at A's in lagging classes.	
	Begin a resume. Format it well and be complete right from the start.	
	Develop a testing plan for the rest of the year.	
Dec.	Solidify semester grades at A's in lagging classes	
	Identify summer programs to target.	
	Consider plans for your story, how you will start to distinguish yourself, and who you will be.	

	Complete a science or social studies fair project or comparable competition.	

Notes:

Spring Semester

Month	Activity	Complete
January	Complete applications for summer programs. Decide which ones are your targets and which ones are your safeties.	
	Reconsider your junior and senior year class selections.	
Feb.	Think about colleges you might be interested in attending and begin to generate a list of options.	
	Plan a school visit or two before junior year, even if they are to schools you are not too interested in, to determine your likes and dislikes.	

March	Identify people and organizations in the community to work with and contact them.	
	Create a plan to prep for AP tests this spring and consider taking SAT subject tests that may align well too.	
April	Prepare for subject tests and AP exams. Aim for subject test scores over 700 and AP scores of four or higher.	
	Decide whether to prep for spring ACT or SAT® this year.	
	Run for leadership positions in your activities and clubs.	
May	Take SAT subject tests and AP exams.	
	Finalize summer plans.	

June	Take your first ACT® and / or SAT® tests if your math preparation is adequate. Be sure to at least do minimal prep for them	
Notes:		

Summer after sophomore year		
Month	Activity.	Complete
	Write a sample essay on the topic: Describe an event or experience that is central to who you are as a person.	
	Update your resume and determine holes to fill in the coming year.	
	Do some summer reading, assigned and otherwise.	
	Continue working to develop your "story."	
Notes:		

2.5 Junior year

Often billed as the most important year of your high school career, junior year will require you to hit your true stride on course rigor and standardized testing. If you have not already taken both the SAT® and the ACT® then do so in the fall. Regardless of when you start, make every attempt to complete your standardized testing by June of this year. If you are in AICE or IB then you will officially enter the program this year and begin their assessments. Remember that the scores on those assessments will also be part of your college application so take them seriously. Scoring high on these tests is a yearlong effort, not something accomplished by cramming a few weeks before.

Fall Semester		
Month	Activity	Complete
August	Register for the PSAT for junior year for National Merit Scholarship qualifying.	
	Watch out for the Tomorrow's Leaders program application.	
	Look for other opportunities for juniors during the school year.	
Sept.	Establish the story that you will present to colleges.	
	Create a profile on the coalition application if you haven't done so already.	
	Prepare for and take the ACT.	
	Attend college fairs to gather information and meet representatives from the colleges you are interested in.	

Oct.	Solidify first quarter grades to get all A's.	
	Prepare for and take the SAT® and PSAT for National Merit.	
Nov.	Solidify semester grades at A's in lagging classes	
	Update your resume and determine if you are missing any components that you can work on this year.	
	Develop testing plan for the rest of the year	
Dec.	Solidify semester grades at A's in lagging classes.	
	Identify summer programs that will deepen your story and gather materials you will need for your application.	
Notes:		

Spring Semester		
Month	Activity	Complete
Jan.	Complete the applications for summer programs.	
	Begin your scholarship search and isolate scholarships to apply for next year. Start creating a list of items you will need for them.	
Feb.	Solidify your college list.	
	Schedule college visits – over spring break, long weekends, summer. Plan to interview on campus if it is an option.	
March	Make contact with coaches at target schools.	
	Make contact with like-minded professors at your target colleges. Try to form a relationship with them based on shared interests or projects that they can help you with.	
	If you are in IB, determine an extended essay topic that will build upon your story and can be submitted to your colleges of interest.	
April	Prepare for subject tests and AP / IB exams. Aim for subject test scores over 700 AP tests over four and IB over 6 if possible.	

	Don't overlook any tests they are all opportunities to distinguish yourself.	
	Identify the teachers who you will ask to write recommendation letters for you.	
May	Take your SAT subject tests.	
	Take your AP and IB exams.	
	Give teachers recommendation request letters before the end of school.	
	Complete the first draft of your IB extended essay.	
June	Take your remaining SAT subject tests.	
	Take your SAT® and / or ACT tests	
Notes:		

Summer after Junior year		
Month	Activity	Complete
	Complete the main essay for the Common Application and / or the Coalition Application.	
	Complete the main essay for state school(s).	
	Redo resume and finalize it, including events and activities that will be added during senior year.	
	Create an ordered list of the top ten activities that you have participated in from your entire resume with a 150 **character** description of each one.	
Notes:		

2.6 Senior year

This is the year when you will successfully complete your college applications. This is the year when the story that you have created is translated into the language of the application. This is the year when you will truly be kicking apps and making your name for yourself. It may also include finishing off your SAT® and ACT testing process if you have not already achieved the scores you need for admissions or scholarships. Depending on the classes you take senior year, this may be the best time to finish off your SAT 2 Subject testing as well.

Much of the time this fall will be devoted to completing applications and all of their associated components. It is important that you select an appropriately challenging schedule for this year as those classes and grades will influence the decisions that college admissions counselors make. In addition, it is imperative to continue to work hard and build on your story throughout this year. If you are deferred from early admission or waitlisted in general admission, your greatest chance of admission will depend on the commitment to your story and the continued excellence that you demonstrate to the selection committee throughout this year. You need to sustain this effort until the end of the year since the AP, IB and AICE exams that you take senior spring will not be used for admissions purposes, but may determine college credits and placement.

Fall Semester		
Month	Activity	Complete
Aug.	Finish your Extended Essay if you are an IB student.	
	Create a matrix to organize all of the essay prompts that you will need to answer.	
	Work on your application essays.	
	Open applications / create accounts for state schools, the Common and Coalition applications. Store your passwords in an accessible location.	
	The first SAT® of senior year is offered this month are you taking it?	
Sept.	The first ACT of senior year is offered this month – are you taking it?	
	Ask for recommendation letters from teachers if you haven't done so already.	

	Create a profile on the Coalition Application and add your target schools.	
	Start to determine your tutoring needs for school subjects.	
	Begin to organize and work on your scholarship applications.	
Oct.	Solidify first quarter grades to get all A's. Remember that colleges will see these.	
	Work on your early applications – early action and decision will go in by the end of this month. The first deadline for some in-state schools like FSU is this month.	
	Complete your FASFA scholarship applications.	
	Complete your CSS Profile scholarship application on www.collegeboard.org.	
	Work on more scholarship applications.	
Nov.	Submit in-state college applications, such as UF.	
	Solidify semester grades at A's in lagging classes.	
	Update your resume.	
	Develop a testing plan for the rest of the year for any remaining standardized tests.	

	Work on even more scholarship applications.	
Dec.	Submit the University of California (UC) applications.	
	Solidify semester grades at A's in lagging classes.	
	Take your final shot at SAT® and ACT® to meet most college admissions deadlines.	
	This month you will hear back from schools for early decision.	
	Work on scholarship applications.	

Notes:		

Spring Semester		
Month	Activity	Complete
Jan.	Complete applications for all remaining colleges.	
	Work on scholarship applications. You get the idea right?	

	Follow up with emails to colleges to confirm application submission and keep yourself on their radar.	
Feb.	Rank order your schools as you await admission decisions.	
	Plan school visits to your target schools to reaffirm your interest.	
	Send care packages with additional materials to support your application to colleges if you have not already done so.	
Mar.	Identify contacts in your potential field of study in the community and contact them to find opportunities for the spring and summer.	
	Create plan to prepare for AP classes this spring. Consider SAT subject tests if they will help with college placement as well.	
Apr.	Prepare for subject tests and AP / IB exams. Aim for subject test scores over 700 AP tests over four and IB over 6 if possible.	
	Finish any remaining scholarship application.	
	Update schools if you are still on waitlists	

May	Take AP and IB exams. Remember that these are for college credit, which means money and placement.	
	Accept offer from school of choice.	
	Finalize summer plans to take advantage of your time.	
June	Last chance at the SAT® and ACT® for Bright Futures scholarships and other state specific aid programs.	
Notes:		

Summer after Senior year		
Month	Activity	Complete
	Get ready for college mentally and physically.	
	Do you need to take any classes to get a head start on college requirements?	

	Can you find any research or job opportunities that will help you develop the skills and knowledge you need in your intended major.	

Notes:

2.7 A closer look at summers

At the start of high school, it may seem like summer is just a necessary break to decompress from the year. After freshman year, very few students and families are thinking about the big picture and college admissions, so that summer is the one that is most often wasted. But remember that there are only three summers during high school! Each one represents an opportunity to work on **making your name** and should be used for exactly that. Students who are successful in the application process make effective use of all three summers and have a plan for how they will accomplish that right from the start. If you have already missed an opportunity to use one or even two of your summers, then there is no point worrying. All you can do is move forward and determine how to best use your remaining summer time.

We suggest that you lay out your high school summers to accomplish three aims. At the beginning of high school, you are still trying to figure things out so the summer after your freshman year should be used for **exploration**. Use this summer to try a few different things and start to really find out what you are interested in. If you already know what your story will be, then jump into it fully this summer. Throughout your sophomore year your story should be starting to come together, so your second summer should be spent with a bit more exploration but you should also begin to **engage** yourself with your story. At this stage, you may need to have a few parallel plans in case some aspects of your primary plan don't pan out. By junior year you should really be putting the pieces together so you should spend your third high school summer fully **assimilating** your story. This is the time when you will start to truly **make your name** and become the story you have created for yourself.

Overall Summer Plan

Freshman Summer	Sophomore Summer	Junior Summer

Since each summer represents a critical opportunity for students to deepen their stories, your selection of what to do is very important. Consequently, a question we always hear is, "What is the best summer activity or program to participate in?" The simple answer is: There is no one best program or activity for students. From summer jobs to summer research, from internships to volunteer work or even educational travel or summer classes, the possibilities are endless. While the options may be overwhelming, students should try to find the excitement in searching for their passions.

This brings us to assessing the value of any one program, which can be challenging. Instead of focusing on a program's content, students and families should focus on three filters when choosing a program:

1. **Selectivity**: If a program is open to anyone who can pay for it, then participating in it doesn't really help a student to stand out. Programs with more stringent admissions criteria help differentiate students. If it isn't selective, then a program should offer value in some other way. If it does then it still may be worth considering

2. **Produced value**: If a program allows students to create something that they will be able to use later in different ways then it has produced value. For example, a science research program that helps students create science fair research projects that they can then use in competition has produced value. Depending on your aspirations this value takes different forms. Want to be a dancer? A summer dance intensive and video of your final performance might be very helpful. For athletes, your specific sports camps may have an impact in the recruiting process. If you need to complete an Extended Essay for IB and your summer program facilitates that, then it has added value.

3. **Personal relevance**: During high school students should be working to create their own personal story. An experience that deepens that story will have value no matter the experience. Again, a loose collection of various experiences will do little to build up your application profile that you present to colleges, but a coherent story will do a lot.

The bottom line is that it is better to do something than nothing. Sometimes circumstances don't allow students to participate in the ideal program but the solution is never to just do nothing. Remember that organic, homegrown programs can be better than any prepackaged offerings that a student might participate in. Ultimately, don't expect that simply paying a lot for a summer experience will be fruitful.

Summer Planning Tool

Dates offered	Program	Value of participation

Are you still looking for other ways to spend the summer effectively? Maybe you have a few programs but still weeks to spare. Wasting away the days still isn't your best option. The key is to understand that time is short and that you need to make the most of each day you have. Here are some other ideas that might interest you:

- Summer reading for pleasure or the book list assigned by teachers
- Summer tutoring to improve your weak areas or get ahead for the following year
- Summer enrichment to deepen your expertise in an area of interest: painting class, photo program, music intensive, etc.
- Summer decompression time so that you are ready for the challenges of the next year

Summer Reading Log

Required reading	
Title	Completion Date

Title	Completion Date

Pleasure	
Title	Completion Date

2. Concluding Thoughts

When you look at all you must accomplish throughout high school it can seem a little overwhelming. That is why it is important to work on these items continuously. Each year in high school has its own purpose and unique set of goals. No matter where you are in your path, you have work to do. The more that you accomplish in the first few years of high school the more prepared you will be for the college application process and everything that takes place senior year. Again, the key to **Kicking Apps and Making a Name** for yourself is not getting to senior year and suddenly realizing how much you have neglected to do during your time in high school.

2. Action Items

❏ If you are starting to use this guide after freshman year be sure to check off the previous years' items

❏ Date items as you do them for future reference and check them off once complete

❏ Be sure to fill in your own items as you complete them as well

❏ Plan your summers:

- Freshman year- Exploration
- Sophomore year- Exploration and Engagement
- Junior year- Assimilation

❏ Prioritize current year tasks and start working on them

❏ Make a pocket sized list of goals and look at them every day: or take a picture of your list and make it you lock screen on your phone

Chapter 3:

Compiling compelling coursework

3.1 Prong 1: Get good grades in rigorous classes

Plain and simple, your grades matter. The key is to recognize that it is not just about the letter grades or the numerical GPA but rather it is about those metrics within the scope of the schedule that you take. When thinking about scheduling, remember that you want to challenge yourself, explore your interests, and make great grades in the process. There is a delicate balance: You need to hit the highest marks possible, but you don't want the classes to be too easy. You should also keep in mind your what ultimate college goals are. If you want to get into the top-tier institutions then, you really need to take the most challenging classes at your school and beyond. If not, then you have a little more wiggle room. In this section, we present some thoughts to guide you through the process involved in scheduling your high school academics.

3.2 Choosing your High School Classes

In most high schools, you will be required to take a relatively prescribed course of studies. Beyond that required core, you will have some choice (and often the core itself is different depending on the program you follow within the school). Even so your schedule will most likely include at least the following:

- 4 years of some kind of English
- 3-4 years of Math
- 3-4 years of Social Studies (usually including World History and US History)
- 3-4 years of Science

Electives will complete your schedule. To prepare for college you should always be progressing towards the next level in each of your core areas of study. Try to do the same in your electives as well. For example:

- 9th grade- English 1
- 10th grade- English 2 honors
- 11th grade- AP/IB/AICE English
- 12th grade- AP/IB/AICE English

Colleges especially value advanced Math, Science, and Foreign Language offerings. You should take four years of Science, Foreign Language and Math at the highest possible level at your school. Colleges view these courses as evidence of higher-level thinking and reasoning ability. The two subjects we call separator classes are Calculus and Physics at the highest levels available. For example, you should always choose Calculus over Statistics because Statistics is in fact an easier course.

Now, take a look at the courses available to you and pick the ones you want to progress in. This is especially important during junior and senior years. Colleges look at those two years as the most important because you are showing your ability to complete college-level work.

Schedule Planner

	9th grade	10th grade	11th	12th
English				
Math				
Science				
Social Studies				
Elective				
Elective				

Example Planner for a competitive student

	9th grade	10th grade	11th	12th
English	English honors	English honors	AP Language	AP Literature
Math	Geometry honors (Algebra 1 honors taken in eighth grade	Algebra 2 honors	Pre-Calculus	Calculus
Science	Biology Honors	Chemistry Honors	AP Chem	AP Physics
Social Studies	World History honors	AP US History	AP Micro/Macro economics	AP US Government/AP comp Government
Elective	Spanish 1	Spanish 2	Spanish 3	Spanish 4/AP Spanish
Elective				

3.3 Choose Your Electives Wisely

Be intentional in choosing your electives. They should be something you enjoy, something to add to your transcript, something related to your intended major, something to add depth to **the name you are making** for yourself. In the eyes of admissions officers, if you are not taking an advanced academic elective, or something that relates directly to your major (e.g. Band for music majors, TV production for film majors, a variety of art classes for design majors, etc) then all other electives are viewed equally. If you going to a highly competitive school, be aware that non-weighted electives can actually drop your GPA, even if you earn an A.

Activity Planner - Complete the Following Lists

Advanced electives offered	Electives related to my major	Electives I want to take
1.	1.	1.
2.	2.	2.
3.	3	3.
4.	4.	4.
5.	5.	5.

These are the classes that you are going to try to fit into your schedule. Think of this as a draft board (for you fantasy football players out there). These are your first rounders for different positions.

At this point you might be thinking to yourself "Aren't we over thinking this? I didn't even put this much thought into my fantasy draft! After all they're just electives. What if I don't get the ones I want?" It is true that you may not get your top choices, but you are now picking electives with a purpose. Completing this chart puts you in control of your schedule. Your draft board is always flexible, but you are being intentional with your selections based on your interests, college and career goals, and academic rigor.

3.4 AP or IB or AICE or Dual Enrollment? That is the question

Parents and students are often confused about which program is best: AP, IB, Dual Enrollment, or AICE, the newest college level course offering. The short answer? It all depends. If attending a two-year school is part of your educational plan, then you should absolutely take dual enrollment courses. In fact, take as many as possible. However, if you're reading this book, you probably have other plans. Dual Enrollment can still be a part of your schedule, but you must be intentional with your selections: Let's look at what each has to offer.

Advanced Placement®

Advanced Placement® (AP) courses are designed by The College Board (the same organization that brings you the SAT®) and have been around the longest of any of the college level high school curriculum options. They cover over the course of a year what colleges typically cover in one semester. The AP curriculum is considered to be very broad, commonly described as an "inch deep and mile wide." These courses are weighted higher than honors courses; college credit is determined entirely by a standardized exam at the end of the year. The exam lengths vary from course to course and feature multiple choice and essay sections. Tests are administered in early May each year, and scores are released in July. Scores have to be sent to the universities directly from The College Board (for a fee of course). You can take AP classes and exams as early as freshman year.

International Baccalaureate®

IB courses are designed by the International Baccalaureate Organization, which is based out of Switzerland. IB is newer than AP but has been around since the 70s. Just like AP, IB is widely accepted in universities in the US. It is also esteemed by colleges around the world. IB courses are also considered to be at a college-level of rigor and generally cover fewer topics more in-depth. IB is focused on the process as well as the product and emphasizes not only the answer, but how you arrived at it. College credit is determined by a combination of an Internal Assessment graded by the instructor and an exam given at the end of the course in early May. Exams, given over the course of multiple days for each subject, are almost entirely free response. IB classes and IB exams are only available to high school juniors and seniors. Students may take individual IB classes for certificates or take their entire course load in IB and earn an IB diploma.

Advanced International Certificate of Education

The curriculum of these courses is designed by Cambridge in England. AICE courses are similar to IB courses: College credit is earned through a combination of an internal assessment and exams. Cambridge's pitch is that AICE allows the student to have more choice in the types of classes they take that count toward the AICE diploma. There are no big end-of-year exams as there are in AP and IB, instead students write three essays throughout the course which are graded to determine college credit. You must check with individual universities for credit policy. You can earn an AICE diploma by "passing" seven classes, four in specific areas and then three additional courses of your choice.

Dual Enrollment

Dual enrollment (the double-edged sword) has, by far, the strongest allure for parents, and understandably so. It has the best sales pitch: guaranteed college credit that also counts for high school credit! Get your high school diploma and your associates degree at the same time! For free! But it also comes with some concerns.

First, as soon as you step into a dual enrollment classroom, your college GPA begins, which can significantly affect you in the future, especially if you do not perform well. If you fail one of these classes, many universities will consider this to be a "college deficit" and will not accept you regardless of your overall GPA. As a result, when deciding whether to pursue dual enrollment classes, it's more important to do well than to do a lot of them. The second concern really has more to do with the student than the program itself. Many times dual enrollment courses are taught at the local community college by actual professors. When you are in a dual enrollment course, for all purposes, you are a college student and treated as such. You are with other college students. You are given the same deadlines, expectations, and responsibilities. You are responsible for approaching the professor with any issues, concerns, problems or questions. You have to meet the professor during their office hours just like any other college student. By law, the college professors and staff cannot talk to the parents, only the students.

To help you decide if dual enrollment is right for you answer the following questions:

1. Is a two-year college part of your educational plan?
2. Is college cost a significant limiting factor for you?
3. Have you taken all of the most rigorous courses available at your high school?
4. Are you definitely going to an in-state university?
5. Are you comfortable making an appointment with a professor during office hours to ask for help that you need?
6. Are you well organized and able to independently complete assignments on time?
7. Do you already know what you want to major in or what career you want to pursue?

If you answer yes to most of these questions then Dual Enrollment could be right for you.

3. Concluding Thoughts

Consider your options carefully when selecting your academic track. Not all programs are equal; not all classes are equal. You have a limited amount of electives, be intentional when selecting them. You should choose your electives based on interest, rigor, and your own sanity and workload. Rigorous classes can come in the form of AP, IB, AICE, and Dual Enrollment. They all have their own strengths and weaknesses as well as their own throngs of supporters and critics. The right choice depends on what your school offers, what your career/college goals are, and your finances. Consider each of these when making your decision. The right choice for you could be a combination of these offerings as well.

3. Action Items

❑ Use the planning tools provided to select your course progression

❑ Get a copy of the electives offered by your school and rank them according to your interest

❑ Decide which rigorous courses you want to take (AICE, AP, IB, DE)

❑ Place these courses into your four-year plan

❑ Keep backups in case your top picks are full or no longer offered

❑ Teachers can make a difference in a course. Find out who the good (not just easy) ones are and do your best to get in their class

Chapter 4:

Max out your standardized tests

4.1 Prong 2: Get High Test scores

Test scores matter. No matter the flaws of any given test, no matter what your personal thoughts are about the validity of standardized testing; test scores matter. Yes there are "test optional colleges," but what does it say about you when you don't submit tests scores to the school you are applying to?

With that in mind you need to determine which test is best for you and how to prepare to maximize your scores. It is true that different schools will emphasize these scores to different degrees but the case can always be made that higher scores will increase your chances of admission to the schools of your choice.

4.2 Basics of the tests

The table below outlines the primary differences between the two main standardized tests, the SAT® and ACT®. While there is some regional preference for one over the other, most colleges will accept either of the tests and you only have to send in your highest scores. Most students are well served to take both.

SAT® vs ACT®

	SAT®	ACT®
Sections	4 sections and an essay	4 sections and an essay
Topics tested	Reading, Grammar, Math	Reading, Grammar, Math, Science
Main challenge	Question difficulty	Finishing in time allowed
Best if	Your math is stronger and you are comfortable with more complex questions	You are fast and your reading is very strong
Scoring	1600 total; add 800 from Reading and 800 from Math subtests	36 total; averaged from 36 each on English, Math, Reading and Science subtests

4.3 Prepping for a Test vs. Answering questions

We hear it all the time, "I've bought my son/daughter all of these prep books and I force him/her to do an hour of practice a night and the scores just don't change." This underscores the difference between simply answering questions and preparing to strategically take the test. Effective test preparation done correctly relies on a few basic principles.

You don't have to prep with a company if you can do it on your own but make sure that however you prep you follow these underlying ideas.

1. You need to **follow a strategic approach**. Never just answer the questions that are given to you.
2. You need to **analyze missed questions to understand why you missed them**. The fact that you missed is significant but why you missed and understanding how to avoid similar mistakes in the future are paramount. After you figure these out, you should redo those missed questions.
3. You need to **score each test you take** so you can see how you are performing relative to the actual test score you are aiming for and adjust your process accordingly.

As you prepare for the SAT®, ACT® or both, you will transition from a robotic question answerer to a strategic test taker and see your scores rise. Remember that a component of any successful test taker's process needs to be review of test content. No matter how smart you are, you can benefit from reviewing math concepts and grammatical rules tested on these tests.

4.4 What other tests need to be on my radar?

Depending on the schools you are applying to, in addition to the SAT® and ACT® you may also need the SAT 2 Subject tests. Remember that your IB, AP and AICE test scores will also help give colleges a complete picture of your abilities within specific subject areas.

SAT Subject tests are offered in a variety of subjects and give students an opportunity to back up their grades with a corresponding test grade. Whether your colleges require these tests or not, every school will look favorably on a student who reports more high test scores. To decide what test is right for you, there are a few questions you should consider:

1. What does my college require? MIT for example requires the Math 2 Subject test and a Science exam.
2. What am I already preparing for? If you are taking an AP test in the spring and studying for it already, why not take the associated SAT Subject test?
3. What am I passionate about? If a particular test would contribute to furthering your story, then it would be worth taking it (even if you need to self-study for it).
4. What tests will make me stand out most? While the Math 1 Subject test is easier, Math 2 would be more impressive.

With so many tests to take, and so much work to do during high school, it is helpful if you can get more bang for your buck by taking additional tests without having to do too much extra.

Test Correspondence

SAT Subject Test	IB class / exam	AP class / exam	AICE class / exam
Physics	HL Physics	AP Physics	AICE Physics AS
Chemistry	HL Chemistry	AP Chemistry	AICE Chemistry AS
Biology (E/M)	HL Biology	AP Biology	AICE Biology AS
Math 1	Algebra 2 Honors	Algebra 2 Honors	Algebra 2 Honors
Math 2	Pre-Calculus	Pre-Calculus	Pre-Calculus
US History	IB History of the Americas	AP US History	AICE US History AS
World History		AP World History	
Literature	IB English 1	AP Literature	AICE English Literature
Languages with listening	IB Spanish 4	AP Spanish, French, German	ACIE Spanish AS
Languages without listening		AP Latin	

SAT language subject tests are offered in Korean, Chinese, Japanese, Latin, German, French, Spanish, Italian, and Modern Hebrew

AP, IB, and AICE tests are all different but they accomplish the same few aims. First they represent another point of distinction for students who can max out the tests. We once worked with a student who didn't get anything less than a 5 on all of her AP tests and a 7 on each of her IB tests. She got into almost all the colleges that she applied to because she showed that degree of excellence. Second, test scores can help you backup your grades. In an era of grade inflation, where over 30 percent of a graduating class may have a 4.0 GPA or better, these test scores validate those grades. Finally they represent another way that you can give colleges a more complete picture of who you are as an applicant and who you will be on their campus.

4.5 Creating a testing schedule

It is never too early to lay out your testing plan. You will likely need to take the SAT® about 3 times and/or ACT® about 3 times. Depending on the colleges that you are interested in you may also need to take SAT subject tests. There are also your standard AP and IB tests to plan each spring. In considering your timing, remember that your math level and development of reading and grammar skills will determine when you can start SAT® and ACT®; testing content knowledge and course selection determines the other tests. Consider the following as well:

- The SAT® reasoning test is usually administered each October, November, December, March, May, June and now in August as well.

- The ACT® is administered each September, October, December, February, April and June and soon in July.

- SAT Subject tests are given on the same dates as the SAT® and you can take up to three on a given date, but the SAT® reasoning test and SAT subject tests cannot be taken on the same day.

- IB and AP tests take place each May.

- The PSAT usually happens in October of 9th and 10th grades and during your junior year is used for the National Merit Scholar competition.

- The PLAN is the pre ACT® and is taken during the 9th and 10th grade years.

Insert the test names and dates for PLAN, PSAT, SAT®, ACT®, SAT Subject tests

Freshman	Sophomore	Junior	Senior

Insert the test names and dates for all AP and IB tests

Freshman	Sophomore	Junior	Senior

As you complete the matrix remember that all of the testing used for college admissions needs to be completed by December of your senior year. Senior fall will be very busy with the rest of the application process, so the earlier you complete tests the better. June of junior year is an ideal target to have completed all of your standardized tests. Take a moment to reassess the planning matrix based on that idea. Make sure that you plan enough time to retake tests as needed and also to take tests at times when they will work best for you. Tests taken at the end of senior year will be important for your IB or AICE diploma, college credit, and college class placement.

4.6 Submitting your scores

Each time you take the SAT® or ACT® you are given the option of reporting the scores directly to colleges. In most cases, we recommend that you wait until all of your testing is done to report them, so you know your scores and can then decide which ones to send to which schools. When you are ready to submit scores you will send your official score reports to your colleges through The College Board and ACT® websites, respectively.

4. Concluding thoughts

Preparing for tests, acing them and sending those scores to colleges will be a critical part of your journey as you **kick apps**! Make sure you plan ahead and schedule your testing dates to your advantage; it is better to over prepare than to under prepare. You would rather have a score or two that you didn't need rather than not being able to apply to your dream school because you hadn't taken a particular test. In addition, remember that these scores are not just for admissions; they validate grades on your transcript and can be used to help you get scholarship money and placement into particular programs at your college.

4. Action Items

- ❏ Use the planning tool to decide which tests to take during which year of high school
- ❏ Find out the dates of the exams you plan to take this year
- ❏ Develop a study plan and timeline for each exam
- ❏ Find study materials and begin your prep

Chapter 5:

Keep records of your accomplishments

5.1 Tracking your progress in official form

As soon as you enter high school you should start keeping track of everything that you take part in and everything that you accomplish. Usually this practice will begin with a simple list of activities. Somewhere during sophomore or junior year, however, it should transform into an actual resume, which should be updated throughout the ensuing years. Your resume will be extremely useful. By organizing your accomplishments and activities continuously, you won't forget anything important that you did.

5.2 Resumes

Never underestimate the importance of a resume. True, everything you put on a resume is somewhere else in your application, but that is kind of the point. You will find this as well when you start applying for jobs. Often, you have to upload a resume and then spend 40 minutes copying lines of your resume into different parts of the application. Still, never underestimate the importance of a resume. Think of your resume as your highlight video: a single page, easy-to-read document that contains you most recent, relevant, and impressive accomplishments. With this document, you have an opportunity to put in front of your admissions counselor or interviewer your very best stuff. As the highlight video, it is most likely the first thing any interviewer or evaluator will look at. Make it impressive, make it stand out, and as with everything else, make it uniquely you.

What should your resume look like? There are hundreds, if not thousands, of resume templates available for free. Below we have provided one that we often recommend, but for the most part choosing between different available styles is just a matter of preference. That being said, there are some basic sections that you should always include.

Heading: Start at the top of the page with your full legal name and current contact information. Students often get in the habit of using their parents' phone number/email address for their primary contact information. Don't do that. You want the person looking at your resume to be able to reach you directly. Don't put down an email address that you never check.

Objective: This is a statement of what you are hoping to achieve with this resume. You should tailor resumes to the specific company or college to which you are applying. Through the application process your objective may change multiple times, double check that you send the correct version to each college.

Work experience: No one is expecting too much here, since you are coming out of high school. A collection of entry-level or summer jobs is perfectly acceptable. Do not include any jobs you left on poor terms. There are three things you will attempt to convey through this section: contacts who can serve as references, dates of employment, and what your responsibilities were. If you want to jazz up your job title a little by calling yourself "a sanitation and facilities specialist" instead of a janitor, go for it. It's not necessarily going to help you, but it could demonstrate creativity.

Education: Include the name and address of the high school you are graduating from and any program or major information. If you were dual enrolled, list that separately and again include any major or track you pursued.

Awards and Honors: List the most prestigious and unique awards and honors first. List the name of the award, why you received it and when you received it.

Activities: Remember these are your highlights, so make sure they are meaningful and relevant to where you're applying. You want to keep the whole resume around 1 -2 pages, so you only have room for what is most important. Good items to include are mission trips, clubs in which you held a leadership role, community projects you are involved in, sports, etc.

Skills: This would include anything that took time to develop. If you received industry certification through a web design class, or drafting, if you have a captain's license, or a rescue diver certification, if you can rebuild engines, can play an instrument, if have performed in plays or musicals, sang the national anthem at the triple A baseball game, etc. Definitely include directly applicable skills, like computer or language skills, but including some other unique skill can at least spark a conversation or pique the evaluator's curiosity in you.

Again, never underestimate the resume. This is your list of accomplishments that you want them to ask you about. It is a simple, straightforward form that can be a huge asset when done correctly and used effectively. It is also your tool to use to fill in other aspects of your applications. On the next page you can see an example of a student resume. What more examples? Find them at **Kickingapps.org**

Name
Address
phone
email

OBJECTIVE

I am hoping to attend a private liberal arts college to earn a 4 year degree in biology as I work towards a career in physical therapy.

EDUCATION

Your High School		2012-2015
International Baccalaureate Program, Advanced Placement		
GPA:4.654	Class Rank:1	Test Scores: SAT®-1920 / ACT-32 (33 super)

ACHIEVEMENTS/HONORS

Regional Science Fair Second Place	2014
Can the Chicken cross the road in the dark?	
State Science Fair Third Place (same project as above)	2014
Regional Science Fair Third Place	2013
Does the age of a residential irrigation well affect its salinity?	
AP Scholar with Honor Award	2013-2015
Chosen to be in the Tomorrow's Leaders Program	2013-2014
County Foreign Language Festival First Place Grammar Test	2012-2014
County Foreign Language Festival First Place Declamation	2012-2014
Tomoka Regional Science Fair Honorable Mention	2011

ATHLETICS/ACTIVITIES

Cross Country	Varsity	2012-2015
By participating in this sport, I learned how to push myself and test my physical boundaries.		
Track and Field	Varsity	2012-2015
Track was a great way to meet new people and stay fit while also experiencing the unity of a team.		
KIVA Lending Team Club	Vice President/Co-founder	2013-2015
Head of selection committee to choose recipients for of $2K in start-up micro loans.		
American Red Cross Club	Treasurer	2013-2015
As treasurer I was responsible for the funds we raised throughout the year that went to the local Red Cross.		
Math Honor Society	Member/Competitor	2012-2015
After being accepted to this club, I participated in competitions in Algebra 2, Pre-Calculus, Calculus, and Statistics winning 3rd place in two different years.		
National Honor Society	Member	2013-2015
This club introduced me to new ways volunteer and be active in the community.		
Spanish Honor Society	Member	2013-2015
Through this club I had to opportunity to tutor students who needed help in Spanish.		

COMMUNITY SERVICE

Sunday School Teacher	120	2012-2015
Responsible for planning lessons, motivating children, and general refereeing.		
Volunteer at Easter Seals	40	2013-2015
Assisted with the therapy sessions for children and keeping them entertained.		
Summer Camp Counselor	140	2013-2015
Camp Dovewood summer camp leader responsible for care of 10 girls and general character development.		

SKILLS

Programming in C++

5.3 The 8 - 10 activities list

For some colleges you will have the option of uploading a resume directly, for others you will be asked to put your resume items into a different form. On the common app this takes the form of the 10 Activities List, on the coalition app it is 8 activities, on some school specific applications you are asked to discuss your most significant activities. In any of these situations, the depth of your explanation within the characters that you are allowed is paramount. If given the option, go in depth on a few of your most significant items and then just list the rest.

5.4 The Awards list

There is a spot on most applications to list your awards. A bit of advanced planning might be necessary to complete this effectively. One of the stipulations on some applications is for them to be "academic awards." Students often have a hard time filling this space, and like anything else on an app, a big blank section says a lot. While not everyone is an academic standout, there is always the possibility to win academic awards if you put yourself in the right position. They are non-athletic distinctions, so maybe entering some different competitions would help: science fairs, national history days, and foreign language festivals are a few such examples. The other option that might work is focusing on the specific subjects you are strong in to win class specific awards. Whatever your plan is, make sure you set yourself up to have content to fill in this section.

5.5 Your digital footprint

Believe it or not, your digital footprint is expansive. With at least 50 percent of colleges and employers doing social media searches on applicants, what you put out into the virtual world will continue to grow in importance. So let us take a moment to consider the importance of (professional looking/sounding) email addresses, social media accounts, and your overall virtual presence. Remember that this is an important consideration throughout high school but also after you receive your admissions decisions. Recent events at top universities have shown that colleges will rescind admission based on social media issues that arise

You are trying to project the best version of yourself. Having email addresses like sexxxxysurferchix or twojointstim420 are probably not going to help you meet that goal. It says something about you. There could be a place for a clever catchy handle, but your college application and resume are not it. If you put a Twitter or Snapchat or Instagram account name in application somewhere, someone will go look at it. Do yourself a favor: Create professional public accounts and make your personal ones private (or better yet delete them altogether). If you really don't want people to see it, then you probably shouldn't post it. For a fresh start check out this article on cleaning up your digital footprint
http://www.zdnet.com/pictures/10-steps-to-erase-your-digital-footprint

Kicking Apps with your Digital Footprint

If many colleges look at your digital footprint, then your primary concern should be how you can use it to your advantage. Use your social media accounts to bring attention to fundraisers you participate in. Post pictures of yourself participating in the school play or marching band or charity event. Post your poem that got an A in your English class for others to see. Your story should come to life through the different modes of social media that you use. So if someone does conduct a search on you, make sure that they get what you want them to get. It is not only a good way to showcase what you do, but it gives you the ability to promote yourself.

Following the right people/organizations can open you up to other opportunities as well. Most universities and professors have gotten onboard the Twitter and Facebook train. A couple of years ago Florida State University was offering a scholarship through a Twitter post. If there is a particular university you want to attend, follow some of its professors, especially those in the department you intend to major in. This can be particularly useful for athletes. Follow coaches and programs, and they will often follow you back. This is your chance to promote yourself and shape your virtual presence to your advantage. For a relatively small investment, you could even create your own website and post all of your images, presentations, activities, awards, and accomplishments.

Run a search on yourself periodically to see what comes up, and then work to make it show what you want. If you spent a couple hours a week purposefully tailoring your internet presence, you would not only know what people can find out about you, but you could control it and make it work in your favor.

5. Concluding Thoughts

In many ways your interests and activities are captured throughout this process. From a print resume to sections you fill in on an app to your digital footprint, you need to put your best face forward and work to impress your admissions counselors with what they see. The resume is often completed almost as an afterthought, but, it is probably the single most referenced document in your application. Take the time to do it right, and it can put you in control of an interview or the first overview of you as a candidate. When you fill it into specific forms for different apps, follow their guidelines, and lead with your best. Remember to plan ahead to have enough to fill into each section. Finally, make your internet presence showcase the best of all you do.

5. Action Items

- ❏ Get together a list of your previous and current employers, their contact information, and your dates of employment
- ❏ List all of the activities you have done: pick the top ones you want to include on your resume and application
- ❏ Make list of any honors or awards you have received
- ❏ Find a resume template that you like
- ❏ If you haven't already done so, create a professional email
- ❏ Take control of your internet presence

Chapter 6:

Which college is right for you?

6.1 Picking the Right School

By now, you should be coming to grips with the intensity of applying to college. And if you are going to put all the time, effort, and money into **kicking apps**, it would only make sense to put some serious thought into what schools you want to apply to.

When students are asked why they want to go to college or what they will go to college for, there is usually an extended moment of silence. They have never really considered why they are going to college, just that they are supposed to. Maybe you haven't considered this either. So take a minute and really think about what you want to gain by going to a university. Go ahead....we'll wait.

Regardless of your answer, remember that you will go to college to get a job. There are a lot great things that happen at universities. They are full of exciting opportunities to participate in cutting edge research, all kinds of interesting people to meet, and all kinds of fun experiences to take advantage of. But at the end of it all, you should graduate with some means of supporting yourself. Some of you reading this guide already know what you were born to do; that can be very helpful in the process. Others may only know that you go to college to get a good job. Where you are on this spectrum will determine what your selection process looks like.

<-->

I have a clear plan   I have an idea   I have no clue

You have no clue. If you truly have no idea why you want to go to college, you need to consider if you really do and where you should start. Think of this in terms of a Return on Investment or ROI. Attending a particular college is going to cost me X dollars per year, and total X dollars. How much earning potential will I have at the end of it? Can I really afford to spend all of that money and hope I figure out what I want to do along the way? Should I attend a two year school instead? Or maybe just work? These are not easy questions, but college is not cheap and you should be intentional about your choices.

You know exactly. Great for you! You have eliminated a large portion of the process. Your search will now focus on finding the schools that offer your intended major. In Florida, everybody wants to be a Gator or a Seminole. UF and FSU are great schools, but if your dream school doesn't offer your intended major, it's not worth applying to much less attending. And that's not all. Something many people don't consider when selecting a university is the importance of opportunities beyond the classroom.

These opportunities are something that we often discuss with students and parents. The conversation can come back to the UF vs FSU debate. Both schools have great political science programs, but only FSU is located in the state capital. The opportunities available there to gain political experience are unmatched in the state.

You have some idea. So you are not exactly sure what you want to do. Do you have a favorite subject? Do you know what you don't want to do? How about where you want to go to college? Often, students who grow up in the south want to move north, and students who grow up on the east coast want to move out west. There seems to be an almost innate desire to go to an opposite climate. Attending an out-of-state university can be very expensive. The idea of snow may not live up to the reality of living and driving in it for months on end. These are all considerations that you can use to help narrow down where you want to apply. If this is you, visiting college campuses can be a big help. Since you're going to live in that community for at least four years, shouldn't you see it before you move there?

There are many different tools that can help guide you through this self-exploration process. If you are not sure what is important to you in a career, a career value score could be helpful. There are a lot of interest inventories that ask you questions and then suggest career options for you. The Myer's Briggs inventory is one of the oldest and most modeled after. If you take the ASVAB, it comes with a similar type inventory. Many states purchase an online career exploration tool that is free for students (Florida's is called Florida Shines). Check with your school counselor to find out what resources are available to you.

6.2 Questions to guide your college selection

Having a target list of schools is a major part of **kicking apps**. It is best to have a target list of four to eight schools; anything less is risky, and anything more and you will have a hard time completing all of the applications effectively. When thinking about what are you looking for in a college, try to answer the following questions:

How many hours do you want to be away from home?

In-state or out-of-state?

Small school or big school? How big is too big? How small is too small?

Do you want to live in a dorm?

What kind of community do you want to live in? Rural? Suburban? Big city?

Do you want to play college athletics? At what level can you realistically play?

What are your financial resources to pay for college?

Are you going to work while you go to school?

What kinds of internships or research positions are you looking for at the school you choose?

Do you want to be a part of Greek life?

What do you want to major in?

Do you want to double major? Minor?

Do you want flexibility to create your own major?

Do you want to attend a faith-based university? Would you be willing to?

The selection matrix below can be helpful in answering these questions and fine tuning your search. Sometimes talking to a guidance counselor or a college consultant can help with this process. Remember that this book is a resource but we are also available to help on a more individualized basis.

Selection Matrix

College selection criteria	Questions to ask	Where to find the answer
Cost	What is the cost of Attendance? What percent of need does the university meet?	University website, do a search for "cost of attendance" and it should come up
Entry requirements	What were the average GPA and ACT/SAT® scores of the current year's entering freshman class?	University website; search for "student profile"
Climate	How different is the climate from what I'm used to?	College visit. Go spend time in the community of the university
Majors	Does it have _____ as a major?	University's admissions website
Internships	How many internships are available? What companies/positions are available? What percentage of interns get hired by the company they intern at?	The best place to get this information is from a representative in the department of your major You could find some information from the university website
Housing options	Are you required to live on campus? What types of housing are available?	Campus tour guide Housing section of website
Teacher/student ratio	What is the average student to teacher ratio (particularly in your major)?	Admissions office Office of the college of your major University website

6.3 Plan your visits

If you are considering applying to a school you should visit it first. Some people wait until they are accepted to visit them, but what if none of the schools feel right? Doing an official tour, seeing the facilities, visiting a class, talking to students, and just generally being present on campus can help you to understand if the school is right for you. An official visit is best and may actually benefit you in the application process. When you visit a school, you should immediately write down your impressions of the visit so that they stay with you. We suggest the following questions to guide you in this reflection:

1. What did you like best?

2. What did you dislike?

3. What was your overall feeling while on campus?

4. What did you think of the facilities? Classrooms? Dorms? Student center?

5. Did you feel like you would have academic resources and support there?

6. Would you fit in with the culture you felt? The students you saw? Describe that culture and those students.

7. What was your impression of the surrounding area? The town, the local terrain, etc.?

8. What were the options you liked for the non-academic side of life? Night life? Non-academic or academic clubs? Activities in the area?

9. Any other things you want to be sure you remember?

Again, write these items down immediately so you don't forget anything. This is really important if you tour multiple colleges in succession. Impressions run together and become muddled if you don't immediately reflect on them.

6.4 Generate a Target List

Once you have educated yourself on your options for schools, you are ready to start coming up with your list. Start by casting a wide net based on the filters above, then pare it down based on really considering what you want in a school. A visit might help to rule out some schools or types of schools. If you cannot visit a particular school, find a similar one close by and visit it for the basis of comparison. Be careful that you aren't just name shopping in this process. The school is the key, not the name of it. As you start to fine tune, then you can generate your target list. Do not apply to just one school, apply to a handful at least.

Break your Target List into four parts as follows:

- **Safety**. 1-2 schools that are 100% certain admissions for you
- **Target**. 2-3 schools that are strong and competitive for your grades, scores, and story
- **High Target**. 1-3 schools that have smaller admissions percentages and place you on the lower end of their admitted students profile
- **Reach**. 1-2 schools that are very challenging but could accept you with a compelling app and crossed fingers

You should have schools on the list that represent a range of admissions possibilities but also all represent options you are satisfied with. If you want to get accurate and detailed information on admissions statistics, look up their admitted students reports to understand what they are looking for in their accepted applicants.

My College List

Classification	Schools
Safety	
Target	
High Target	
Reach	

6.5 Finalizing your Target List

Ultimately, you don't need to have a final list of schools until you finish all of your apps. The key is to develop a core list early and work toward that with the flexibility to apply to more along the way. Remember to be honest with yourself throughout the process; there is no sense in overreaching and coming up empty. Also, keep the list under control. If you shoot for too many schools, you will submit a lot of mediocre apps instead of a more select list of really strong ones. Also keep in mind the importance of really knowing the schools you are applying to. We often hear comments like "I plan to apply to all of the Ivies," which reveals that the applicant may not understand that there are key differences between all of the Ivies and how those differences extend to the type of students each one looks for. A student who is an ideal candidate for Dartmouth, for example, may not be exactly who Harvard is looking for. The eventual app you submit to different schools will probably need to be different to maximize your chances of admission.

6. Concluding thoughts

Where you choose to attend college will have an effect on you personally, professionally, and financially- so be as intentional as possible. Make deliberate decisions about what schools you want to apply to and why. Don't just apply to Harvard because it is highly regarded. Apply there because attending will benefit you in some specific way. Put as much thought into your first choice as your last. Find out as much as you can about the schools and the programs they offer. Visit them. It is just as important to find out that you absolutely don't want to live in a particular area as anything else. You just saved yourself a lot of time and money.

6. Action Items

- ❏ Start a conversation with your parents about finances for college
- ❏ Identify possible careers or career fields
- ❏ Start visiting colleges, begin locally and branch out from there
- ❏ Think about businesses or organizations that you would like to work for and find out where they get their interns from
- ❏ Create a college list with a balance of school and acceptance percentages

Part 2:

Your story & how to best showcase it

Chapter 7:

Completing your applications

7.1 Prong 3: Making your name known to universities.

Up until now we have been working through how to prepare yourself to shine in your college apps. Now we get into the apps themselves. To start, there are many different types of applications for different universities. So let's explore them.

Completely University-Based Applications

This is becoming less common, but since universities still have their own application embedded in their website. The benefit of this is that you are submitting your application directly to them. You can tailor your application to them specifically (personal statements, achievements and activities important to them, resume, etc.) and your information goes directly to their in-house system. You don't have to worry about lag time between when you upload or complete a section of an application and when the university receives it. Generally, you will create a profile, get assigned a student ID, and pay your application fee. Then you simply fill out their application and upload supporting documents to them. It's clean, it's simple, and there are fewer eyes on your information (for those of you concerned about privacy).

Third party mass application sites

More and more universities are outsourcing their applications to organizations like the Common Application (Common App) or the Coalition for Access and Equity. These are the two major sites, and both promise the same thing, a one stop shop for college applications. You complete one application, and then you can submit that application to as many of their member universities as you want. There may be additional school-specific information or supplemental essays and materials that the individual universities want, but for the most part you get to complete the application one time (which can be a major time saver). You then select the universities you want to apply to and pay each university's application fee, and then the university can access your information. Again, while this is a nice feature, you do lose some of the school specific tailoring, but if you are applying to several schools that accept the same third party application, it is worth it. You can also still submit different versions of your application to different schools if you choose to. For example, on Common App you can change your main essay for each school you apply to.

Student Academic Reports

This is not really a different application method per se, but this seems like an appropriate time to discuss it. A current trend among colleges is to have students manually enter their academic record (transcript) and then the college or university will only request official transcripts for students they accept. The Common App and the Coalition for Access and Equity have these features as part of their respective sites, and there is also a separate company that puts out the Self-reported Student Academic Report (SSAR). Accuracy in completing these is critical. Any discrepancy, intended or not, can cause your acceptance to be immediately revoked. Get a copy of your transcript from your school and copy it exactly as you see it into the site.

7.2 The Common App

As discussed earlier, the Common App allows students to complete the parts of the application that all their member universities have in common. In addition, these universities have agreed to accept the Common App essays as their application essay. Completing the Common App can be time consuming so you will want to get started early. Students can complete the profile sections before senior year to save time in the process. As soon as the Common App resets (usually August 1st) you should be completing your school specific content. Most years the main essay prompts are available before the summer so you can start work on those before you complete the rest of the app.

Student Profile: This section is composed of your demographic information and your general academic history. You might find it useful to have a copy of your transcript to reference while completing this section.

Essays: The Common App gives you multiple essay prompts which are generally released in the spring. The application goes live in late summer for the fall admissions cycle. You're going to want to complete and revise (as many times as necessary) essays for at least two of the prompts. Some universities will also have supplemental essays as part of their individual section of the application.

Recommenders Section: There is a section for your high school counselor to complete and there are also teacher recommendations. Do not assume that just because you put in someone's email and information that they received the invitation to provide information about you. Follow up with them. Recommendations make up a critical component of the application and you should treat them as such; we will return to discuss them further later on.

Self-reported academic history: To keep pace with their competition, the Common App is adding a section for you to enter your academic history on your own. Similar to the SSAR (Student Self Academic Report) it is designed so that colleges and universities can make their decisions without having to rely on official transcripts. You put in your academic history, and they only request transcripts for students they accept.

Collaborator enhancements: This feature allows other people to view application progress and documents as collaborators. We advise against it. The idea is that you can invite someone to essentially help you with your app which is a bit of a red flag. While colleges are aware that students can receive help from companies like ours, they don't know who does. If this feature is shared with universities, then they could hold it against you or doubt that the work you put forth is your own. If you want to share something with someone for feedback, it is just as easy to email them a copy or print it out and bring it to them.

7.3 The Coalition App

The Coalition for Access and Equity is a relatively new third party application site. It is a little more modern than the Common App, but functions in relatively the same way. Some of the newer features of the Common App were first offered by the Coalition App (the academic self-report and collaborator options).

Profile: The student profile is very comprehensive, but like most of the Coalition app it is very user friendly. You will input your basic demographic information, activities, awards and your academic history here as well. There are sections for you to put brief descriptions of activities and interests, which are similar to what you would find on a resume: single descriptive sentences. Unlike Common App, the Coalition requires users to complete the profile before starting school specific content.

Locker: This is a place to save all your documents that you submit as part of an application. You can edit them, store them, and allow others to view them and make suggestions. Think of this as the Coalition's version of Google Drive. It makes it convenient to access frequently used documents for applications as well as for editing from places other than your laptop or home computer.

7.4 When to apply

Some of the decisions about when to apply are easy. For example always submit your application on time, or ahead of time. Make sure that all of your extra materials (including letters of recommendation and sometimes even scholarship forms) are also submitted on time. For best results consider that "on time" means one to two weeks ahead of deadlines to allow for any issues that might arise and show that you are really interested in their college. You never know, for example, if you will lose your internet connectivity the night before the app is due or if a hurricane will hit at an inconvenient time.

The question of when to apply is easy if your target college only has one admissions deadline or if you are committed to applying regular decision. But if you decide to apply early you have some more choices. The two main early application options are early decision (ED) or early action (EA). Understanding the differences between them is important when making this decision.

Early Decision
- ED is a binding early application option and is exclusive- you can only apply to one school ED.
- You may apply for regular decision to other school's but you agree that if accepted ED you will withdraw all other apps and accept that school's offer of admission.
- ED acceptance rates are often double the regular decision rates at selective schools and you will know that you are accepted by December.

- You are committed to that school regardless of financial aid awards or any other considerations.
- You might also be giving up the chance to hear back from multiple schools and weigh the options against one another. In essence, you weigh your options first and that's why you apply early.

Early Action
- For EA you can apply early and find out early about admission decisions, but you can usually apply EA to multiple schools.
- You are not bound to attend that school and can wait to hear back from your other schools before making a final decision.
- You may get a slight bump in the percent chance of admission, but it usually isn't as great as the bump for ED.

In addition, you may find some schools offering ED1 and ED2; this just means that there are two different dates to apply the same way. Sometimes EA is offered as a single-choice option (restrictive early action), which means you cannot apply to any other schools EA but you can apply regular decision. It is best in any of these cases to fully read the expectations of the type of application you select before you commit to it. When you make an early decision commitment you will be asked to sign a form and send it in to indicate that you agree to their terms.

IF YOU DO DECIDE TO TAKE AN EARLY APPLICATION ROUTE, EVEN A RESTRICTIVE ONE THAT LIMITS YOUR ABILITY TO APPLY TO OTHER SCHOOLS, REMEMBER THAT YOU STILL WANT TO COMPLETE ALL OF YOUR OTHER APPS JUST IN CASE. The worst scenario with an early applicant is getting rejected in early December and then having only two weeks to turn around all of your other apps.

Deadlines for your Target List Schools

Rank	College Name	Regular Decision	Early Decision	Early Action	Other

In the table above, Rank indicates your ranking of the choices. Put in all of the deadlines and then circle the deadline that you will shoot for at each school. Remember that regardless of the deadline you should try to submit all materials two weeks ahead of time to ensure that your materials get there. In addition, confirm the receipt of all materials with a call or email following your submission.

7.5 Understanding your essay prompts

Regardless of which application portal you use, or if you apply through the school-specific site, for many colleges essays are a significant part of the application. Before you dive headlong into answering the essay questions and clicking submit, it is worth taking some time to really understand the task that is presented to you in each essay prompt and making sure that you answer it effectively. Most topic ideas can be tailored to fit many different prompts, but you do need to be sure that your essay answers the question being asked. Begin by reading each essay prompt, and then underline the specific parts of the question that you need to answer and consider how you will divide your response to accomplish that task. We call this process "unpacking."

Let's look at an old example from Florida State University to demonstrate the process of unpacking an essay prompt. Take a look at the essay below:

> *We firmly believe that every person is unique and of value. Our University is enriched by embracing individual differences and creating a community that is much more than the sum of its parts. In 650 words or less, share your story with us. Tell us how you came to be the person you are today, and about your passions and future expectations. Describe how you will benefit from our community and how our community will benefit from you.*

Now look at how it would be unpacked.

> *We firmly believe that every person is unique and of value. Our University is enriched by embracing individual differences and creating a community that is much more than the sum of its parts. In 650 words or less, **share your story with us**. Tell us **how you came to be the person you are today**, and about **your passions and future expectations**. Describe **how you will benefit from our community** and **how our community will benefit from you**.*

So, in 650 words, admissions officers are expecting you to address five different aspects of this prompt. In essence, they want you to tell "your story" and show that you know their college and how you connect to it. While the story is clearly the most important feature, showing that you know the school makes them more confident that you are serious about attending and not just throwing in an application for fun.

Before you jump into writing- really before you even decide which prompt to answer- you should probably begin by unpacking the prompts and looking at all of the parts of a given essay. Use this table to focus your brainstorming:

Unpacking your Prompts

Application	Points to address	Ideas

7.6 Additional information

In some applications, like the Common App and many more, you have the option of writing an extra essay or adding "any additional information." In these cases, the best choice is always to do it. Just choosing to write something extra- and especially writing another strong essay- will increase your candidacy for admission, particularly to the more selective schools. View this as an opportunity not a chore; you have the chance here to give the admissions counselor a more complete view of you and more compelling reasons to accept you.

7. Concluding Thoughts

Completing college applications is a time-consuming process that will move much more quickly if you have all of your information organized and easily accessible. You can apply to colleges either directly or through a third-party website like the Common App or the Coalition App. When completing your apps really think about what you are being asked to include and provide them with thoughtful responses. Every word you write is important and every essay that you draft could make or break your application. Try to create an application of very even quality, one that consistently shows mastery and excellence and doesn't have anything that would give them reason to question your candidacy.

7. Action Items

❏ Get a copy of your transcripts

❏ Identify the location of the application for the universities you want to apply to

❏ Identify people who can not only write a good recommendation for you, but also one that will be different from your others

❏ Create a Common App, Coalition App, and SSAR account.

❏ Create a professional email and social media accounts and flood them with positive things

Chapter 8:

Writing an app-kicking essay

8.1 How do I write an APP-KICKING essay

The million-dollar question in the entire application process is, What makes a great essay? To begin to answer this question, it helps to think about what the essay tells the college. That can be boiled down to two elements.

1.   **Why will you be a good addition to the school (what makes you unique)?**

2.   **How intelligent are you?**

You should, therefore, tailor your essay to tell your story in an engaging and compelling way. A great essay usually approaches this task from one of two trajectories: describing a uniquely interesting experience or conveying a somewhat mundane experience in a powerful and enlightening way. You could even do both. It is critical, right from the start, to understand that what you are working on is really important and that every single word you choose will matter- but at the same time, understand that this is a process and that in early drafts you may have very little "right." Give the process enough time and thought to transform a writing sample to a great essay; it may require you to step away from an essay for periods of time before coming back to it or to completely scrap an entire essay a few drafts into the process if it isn't going anywhere.

8.2 The Process

There are many college essay guides that give students examples of winning essays. Our approach is a bit different: We hope to provide those resources as well, but our primary focus is the process. What you will see below are the first drafts of selected essays followed by the finished products. Evaluate the first drafts and understand what is and is not effective about them, but then also understand what needed to happen to make them effective in their final form. An **App Kicking** college essay is not crafted the night before the application is submitted. It is the result of careful planning and consideration of the essay- from understanding the prompt to determining the essence of your message to drafting to finally crafting the ideal response.

Jumping right into a draft can be the biggest mistake that students make. Again, essay writing should be a deliberate process. Brainstorm many topics, outline multiple options, draft, redraft as many times as it takes, and then eventually finalize. It is a good idea to have multiple pieces of writing to choose from and consider submitting different essays to different schools if some fit better than others.

Topic Selection & Brainstorming

Ideally, this process should start long before the essay needs to be done. Give yourself time. Talk to your friends, family, teachers and coaches about potential topics. Think about what would be interesting to readers: what would engage them and make them want to know more about you? Those are the kinds of characteristics that make great essays. Something that you are really passionate about and love to write about will end up much better than something you just think that admissions officers will want.

Use the Space below to Brainstorm some topics:

Outlining

In the traditional strictly structured sense, outlining doesn't have much of a place in the college essay writing process. We suggest using something more functional: a working outline. Start by dividing a document into three sections- Introduction, Body, and Conclusion- and then list all of the topics that would be good to include in each of those areas. Once you have that list, just start writing anything you can think of under each idea. This writing should be stream of consciousness- just get the content on the page. Let the essay sit overnight and then revisit it the next day. Add new ideas to each section but also start to cull out the key elements. This is the stage to distill your essay down to a central point, to find the essence of your message.

What follows is an example of a working outline we developed with one of our students. In this case, the student wrote a full draft that needed to be refocused and developed in the right direction. The deep outline helped the student with both of those. Student HT was a great swimmer and also passionate about math; she wanted her essay to show the connection between these two disparate worlds.

Deep outline example

1. Relevant ideas to include
Central image = Bridges
Connection of the two parts of you Math and swimming

Swim / water sports – distance freestyle and backstroke
Favorite non swimming water sport is sailing – freedom of sailing 2 people in the boat
Getting hit by the boom – concussed
        Clumsy on land – grace in water

I'm good at math but I'm not an SAT® 800 genius Indian math kid – but I like it
Math nerd – atypical math nerd

I like swimming and I'm good but not great
Hard worker – willing

2. Intro
I should have been a mermaid. Not so much because of the swimming ability though my state championship. But it's the part right when the mermaid gets out of the water and loses her tail, she tries to walk and inevitably falls… That's me. Water is my escape, the place where gravity – of situations etc loses its grip on me
Can we bring in the bridge up here- between water and land

As I race my mind clears and there is nothing but the movement of my body in the water, I'm flying above my cares, my Spanish vocab, my….

Though I love the water, the thrill of competition in the pool the freedom I feel is really when I sail

Math in swimming?

Describe sailing

I like to be active when I am out on the water my perspective changes and I see the true beauty in things

Sailing and sailing (mind open and broadened) under a bridge and then into the idea of bridges – navigating under a bridge and then your reflection on the bridge

3. Body

Talk about swimming

5:00 am practice and rushing to school to catch the bus to the math competition. I throw my hair up in a ponytail and run out stinking of chlorine, the math competition starts in 45 min. My mom looks at me in the car – did you see the time you just swam? -

Bridge again? Math and swimming bridge – how are you a bridge between those

Talk about math competition

Fear at math competitions – thought you had to be a genius. They take it seriously like pre swim meets and headphones on getting psyched up.

I thought it would be fun to do – wanted to see what it would be like and then really liked it, while I'm not really competitive about it I value the fact that these kids are really into it and competitive about it

They go home and practice 2 hrs. of math and I go swim for two hours

Student athlete bridge – some kids I swim with think they can swim at Harvard but they would sink there

Sailing is up in Maine now not able to do it as much as I once did

Don't have to practice to be good at it or enjoy it – not very competitive at it

4. Conclusion

How do we bring mermaids back –

In lore of mermaids – they all want to be human, but then it isn't all it is cracked up to be

I may be awkward on land and graceful in the water but I enjoy both aspects of myself

Or bridges or something

You can see that she wrote the outline without much organization; it was simply a way to get the ideas on the page and then start to put them together. This is a deeper brainstorm, free from the constraints of paragraphs but an essential bridge between the topic selection and the actual draft. You can see HT's starting and ending essays at

www.kickingapps.org

Drafting

You should be able to distill your essay into a single sentence which will become the essence of your writing and reflect a core aspect of your identity. In choosing this thesis sentence, think about the character traits that you want to convey. Focus on those that you feel most strongly about and can address with the most passion. Do not try to describe everything that makes you unique; this will distract the reader and dilute the quality of your essay. Six-hundred fifty words is not enough to do that well. Throughout the writing process, it is helpful to go back to the basics and re-establish your focus on this essence. Eventually, if the essay is written well, that idea will end up in the conclusion as the last thing the admission counselor reads about you.

Answer this question in one sentence: How did your _____ change you? Then attempt to craft an essay so that this will be the conclusion left in the reader's head after as he or she finishes reading your essay.

If you do all of this correctly, you will be able to separate your essay into two sections: before and after your experience. The narrative will be your tool to convey your message so the reader ends up knowing you on a deeply personal level. Do not be afraid to lay everything out for them; in fact, the only way they will connect with you is if your writing makes them feel something. The reader wants to know about your dreams and aspirations, why you view the world a certain way, how you react to adversity, and other things that explain the unique perspective that you will bring to campus.

8.3 Mechanics of the essay

There is no correct formula for the essay; in fact, different approaches work better for different topics and different applicants. Into theater? Maybe writing your essay as a screenplay would be good. Into computer science? Try writing part of your essay in code. Skilled in a foreign language? Consider writing an essay or parts of your essay in a different language. Regardless of your approach, the general setup of most essays will still be an introduction, a body, and a conclusion. What you do in each section is incredibly important, especially when you remember that your essay is just one of many being read. How will yours stand out to a person reading hundreds each day?

Introduction

You need to immediately hook your reader. If you don't get their attention (or worse, if you turn them off right from the start), you are going to have a hard time ever getting them back. Consider starting amid the action of the essay instead of dragging the reader through a slow lead up. If you are writing about a car accident in your childhood, you don't want to start with your birth or even the morning of accident itself. The best hook might be to write about the point of impact between your car and the tree.

Consider the following pairs of opening sentences. How does each one grab you? Which ones would make you want to keep reading?

Example A1: When I was in first grade, I decided to sell mini books that I had created.

Example A2: In elementary school I ran an empire, employed half of my classmates and was living the high life.

Example B1: Growing up with two older sisters was always an adventure.

Example B2: As the caboose of a crazy train of three sisters, I am often referred to as "the baby" among family.

Example C1: My science fair project on microbial fuel cells was the first time I really did science.

Example C2: I am going to make people give a shit; they already take it, plenty of it, but pending more research, microbial fuels may eventually power water purification systems and much more.

Example D1: Growing up as a tomboy my fascination with power tools never struck me as odd.

Example D2: The deafening buzz of the power saw filled my ears as I carefully cut along the black sharpie line under the watchful gaze of my father.

Example E1: I do not have a specific section of the plane that I like best, but I do prefer the window to the aisle seat.

Example E2: Buckling my seatbelt, I breathe out the stress of schoolwork left behind. The smell of luggage, airplane fabric, and a hint of the food court fills my lungs, increasing my excitement for the journey ahead.

In each pair, you see a mundane and then a more interesting and impactful approach. Again, this is the first impression you make on an admissions officer, so spend time fine tuning your hook. Don't be afraid to rewrite it several times. Make it count!

Body
The body needs to have a flow to keep the reader engaged and develop your story. It is where the action in your story will take place; every story worth reading needs to have some sort of action and resolution. If nothing happens, it is hard to make it interesting. In other words, don't just hold their interest- engage your reader, captivate them with your story, make them want to know more. The organization of your paragraphs can help you achieve this. Again, remember that your words are limited, so use each one carefully. The challenge is to neither be too broad nor too narrow, an outcome which will take some revision to perfect.

Conclusion

This will be the part of your essay that the admissions counselors read before making a decision about your admission. This section, then, is as important- if not even more important- than the hook in the introduction. The conclusion is where you will attempt to convince them to accept you. We have worked with students who have rewritten their concluding sentences dozens of times to make them exactly right. The essence of your essay and, in fact, the essence of you will likely end up as the final sentence. Remember that you will be selected for admission to a college based on who you show them you are. As you write the conclusion, consider this question: Who do you want the reader to think you are once they finish your essay?

Here are some examples of concluding sentences. What does each one tell you about the applicant?

Conclusion 1: As I lace up my now-browned sneakers, I continue my hike to FSU to learn the vital skills of modern medicine and pursue my dream.

Conclusion 2: I am now comfortably a *calculated* artist, a dancing oxymoron.

Conclusion 3: Like the proverbial apple that hit Newton's head, this experience catalyzed a rapid spike in the level of my academic inquiry: I now try to fill every gap of time in my day with opportunities to further expand my knowledge, whether that be by working on an AP Bio class online or learning how to speak Spanish through CDs played in my car.

Conclusion 4: Through all of the turbulent times in my life I have remained calm and focused, like a ship holding its course through a storm. I was forged with unfathomable strength so that I could accomplish what at first seemed impossible.

Conclusion 5: But I already knew who I was. I didn't need anyone to tell me and I didn't need to figure it out. It was just something I learned in my pajamas.

Now think about your own conclusion. Don't rush it; try to think of several different options. In the table below, write your current conclusion sentence. Then take time over the next few days to write some other versions of it.

Your Concluding Thought

Start:

8.4 Some examples

The examples below typify what we consider to be exemplary essays. The point for you is to explore the transformations they went through. To use this guide most effectively, read the original drafts, comment on them yourself, and then read the final versions. Think about their improvement as you draft, edit, and finalize your essay.

Sample 1:

Original essay RB

Prompt: *Common App- Some students have a background, identity, interest, or talent that is so meaningful they believe their application would be incomplete without it. If this sounds like you, then please share your story.*

    I am sitting here at the park during another sweltering Florida summer watching my sister and brother enjoy strawberry ice cream cones as they drip all over their faces and down their arms. Despite my vow to veganism there will always be a special place in my heart for ice cream. Admittedly it is my favorite food. I grab the hem of my vintage Grateful Dead shirt and wipe my sisters face in lieu of a napkin. I lick the remains off my hand and the sweet taste seems to take me back to time not so long ago but to what feels like an eternity.

    2001 was an eventful year in my despite my vague recollection of it. My Deadhead parents decided I was old enough and we could now hit the road again. So they packed up and shoved me, my purple stuffed dancing bear, and our dog Samson into the big ugly blue GMC van for a cross country journey that would inevitably set the course for the rest of my life.

In order for this story to be properly told I feel it is best to give you a brief history on the nut cases that are my parents. My parents met on dead tour when they were 18 they spent the next 8 years of their lives on the road until 1999 when I was born. The birth of their love child was obviously the best day of their lives and they then settled to in Arizona to raise their beautiful baby girl. But wanders will continue to wander and not but two years later they were back on the road with some new company, me.

The journey started and we headed to Colorado. We spent some time in Colorado where I met a lot of interesting people. There were never many kids around when I was growing up, but it was okay because all the adults acted like children anyway. The running joke was that I was doing a great job raising my parents. I was never treated as a child I was just another person who had ideas and things to contribute. Of all the vague memories I have the one that is very prominent is how I would draw pictures for the people I would meet on the road. Drawing has always been my outlet and growing up around various stoned hippies was the perfect support system. Dancing, laughing, music and art are all part of the Deadhead culture that even after the death of Jerry never went away. No matter where we went there was always a sense of community compiled of individuals each more unique than the last.

We made our way across to Pennsylvania stopping anywhere interesting along the way. My dad was one of those travelers who was truly focused more on the journey more than the destination. That has greatly influenced me through out my life. Focusing more on the moment and what you can learn and get out of it than rushing to finish. I think thats a lot like painting. Each brushstroke is important in its own respect and a conglomerate of brush stokes makes a Picture. Yes there are brush strokes that went askew but in the end a masterpiece isn't a masterpiece without a few mistakes. I really digressed there what was I saying? Anyway we made it to Pennsylvania eventually. In Pennsylvania my dad's best friend owned an ice-cream company and my mom, my dad, and I were going to be traveling icecream salespeople.

The ice cream business is booming. On a hot day no one can resist the delicious treat and of course it was all homemade and organic. We had a trailer which we sold ice cream out of and we would travel to various festivals and concerts and sell ice cream. I would help take orders and scoop ice cream, but my favorite job was trying all the flavors and making posters. Selling ice cream was great but it's a very seasonal business. As the summer closed so did our trailer and we headed to North Carolina.

Big shocker we spent a lot of time living in Asheville with various friends and interesting people, and as we loaded up the van to go to a new destination I told my dad something that he probably resented me for the rest of his life.

I said, "Daddy, I don't really want to move around anymore I want to have a home... I want to go to school."
And thats what we did. We found the little town of New Smyrna Beach in Central Florida and they bought a house and settled down. As years went on they had two more kids who are the loves of my life and my best friends. I did I great job raising them too. It is all bets summed up by the Jerry Garcia himself when he said, "What a long strange trip it has been"

Your feedback

What is good about the essay?

What is bad about the essay?

What is the essence of the essay?

What would you do differently to make this an App-Kicking essay?

Other comments:

Final essay RB- admitted ED Middlebury

A smile touches my lips as I watch my younger siblings enjoy the simple pleasure of ice cream on a hot Florida day; my responsibility for them fades into an appreciation of the moments we spend together. The sticky remnants of what was once the frozen treat soon covers their faces, hands, and even makes its way into their glowing blonde locks. I grab the hem of my vintage Grateful Dead tee and wipe my sister's freckled face. Despite my reservations about the dairy industry, I steal a lick of my brother's cone. The sweet taste brings back bittersweet memories, of what seems like ages ago.

Our big blue GMC van (Or as I affectionately called it "The Mystery Machine") bops down the winding highway towing the teal trailer filled with every flavor of ice cream you could imagine. There are people I don't know sitting next to me; they seem nice despite their visible layer of grime and lack of commitment to hygiene. I peer to the front seat at my mom with her long flowing hair and peasant dress and my dad with his scruffy beard, and tie dye. They're a picture perfect pair and my small hands begin sketching them as they all chat. The lines are shaky and the proportions are all wrong but my mother tells me she loves it. If only we had a fridge to put it on.

I had been on the road since I was two, traveling around with my Dead Head parents, dog Samson, and our ice cream business on wheels: Lilybells. We stopped at music festivals around the country to sell the culturally unifying delicacy to the free spirited, stoned, and always interesting people of the road. As my parents danced about filling orders, I would sit and draw the unfamiliar faces as they passed. Our life, simply put, was different. When most children received teddy bears I received dancing bears. Instead of story time at the library I enjoyed folk singing at the drum circle. My father would strum his guitar and sing me to sleep with Ripple, and I'd open my eyes in the morning greeted by an entirely new place.

This was my life and I learned many things I'll never forget. Like the importance of keeping track of your shoes, how meat is murder, and that spinning in circles qualifies as dancing. My childhood party trick was knowing all the words to "The Big Rock Candy Mountain". But as I grew older I knew something was missing, and there came a day when my dad and I were sitting in the shade of the Trailer sharing a strawberry ice-cream cone. The sticky remnants of ice cream dripped onto my hands and covered my face, and as my dad grabbed the hem of his Grateful Dead Tee to wipe my face I said something uncharacteristic. "Dad I don't want to move around anymore. I want a home."

My father had always said, "We are houseless not homeless" which is a convoluted way of playing into that cliché about home being where the heart is. While I try to live a life devoid of bad clichés, admittedly I see truth in that. We were happy on the road and those experiences formed the colorful foundation of my character. But there is something to be said for having a physical place in the world. Surrounded by chaos you just want to know you fit in somewhere, that there is a place that you can always return.

As we settled into our life in Florida nothing has ever really become less chaotic (in some ways, on the days I care for my siblings, it has become more so) but I find peace in the fact that my drawings are displayed on the outside of the freezer door and on the inside there's still a pint of strawberry ice cream.

Sample 2:

Original essay AN

Prompt: *Common App- Discuss an accomplishment or event, formal or informal, that marked your transition from childhood to adulthood within your culture, community, or family.*

I looked around the empty room recounting all the lifelong memories I had made in just 6 short days. I sat patiently on the foot of my bed, waiting for the kids to walk in the door as they did on the first day giving me a hug, ready to have the best week of their whole entire year, but they didn't come. I scanned the four beds that were occupied by those kids just an hour ago, but there were no little bodies wrapped in a blanket like a burrito to be seen. Tears began to roll down my face as I thought of the friendship we had built from when their parents dropped them off to when their parents picked them up. Faster and faster the tears came as I remembered our chicken fights in the pool and how they made me laugh with their corny jokes. Soon my tears became a waterfall feeding a pool of water on the ground as I realized that the next time I see them some of their conditions will have progressed, leaving them in a wheelchair. At that moment on the foot of that bed, in that room, in that cabin, at that MDA Summer Camp I realized that I wasn't a kid anymore.

There is something about seeing a room full of kids bound to wheelchairs, having trouble walking, or going to be in one of those states soon that will change a person, especially a privileged kid with no real problems to face in his life like me. Being a caretaker for someone, let alone a child with muscular dystrophy, forces a person to conform to the mold of adulthood given that one has to learn the characteristics of sacrifice, relentless hard-work, patience, physical but more importantly emotional strength, compassion and so many other qualities that allow you to be a person's lifeline. When I read the email from the Muscular Dystrophy Association saying that I was chosen to be a counselor at their camp I knew that it was going to be a challenging experience, but to me it seemed like nothing too different from the countless Embry-Riddle basketball camps I had coached or the numerous hours I had spent with the kids in the Remar orphanage during my mission trips to El Salvador. However, after reading my camper's file and talking to the other counselors in my cabin about their kids the night before camp started, I came to the realization that it was going to be one of the most demanding weeks of my life.

The nervousness that overtook me when I looked into the eyes of the parents that trusted me with the being they created and treasured most in their lives, their son, was crippling. For 6 days I was going to be the figure in his life that he trusted the most, the one that cared for him, the one that put him to bed at night, and the one that he counted on for everything. Luckily, my camper's condition had not progressed to the point where he needed assistance with everything so I was put into a position to do what I love to do, help others Throughout that week I became the arms and legs for some of the campers. These children needed assistance with everyday routines we take for granted: getting out of bed in the morning, getting their clothes on, going to the bathroom, getting in the pool, taking a shower, and brushing their teeth. The only thing these kids had control over were their electronic

wheelchairs, their words, and their smile, but that is what differentiated them from me.
 No matter what glistening smiles always occupied their face and words of kindness and appreciation echoed out of their mouth. I learned that life isn't fair and that fate can be a terrible thing, but that didn't stop these kids. They accepted that life had put them at rock bottom and their fates were in the hands of their terrible diseases, but they were going to be an inspiration for others. In this case it happened to be me.

In life, there is no one event or person that makes you an adult, but there are events and people that form the foundation of who you are in adulthood. The reason why I am the patient, caring, loving, strong, mature man I am today is because of that camp and because of those kids. Without them I would not appreciate my family, health, and life like I should. Without them I wouldn't have an inspiration to be the best person I can and strive to initiate change in the world. Before I left for camp, my mom told me that I was going to be a blessing to the kids at camp, which I believe I was, but I never could have imagined how much of a blessing those kids were to me. I walked out of that camp on that sunny Florida summer morning not the kid I came in as but the man I am today.

Your feedback

What is good about the essay?
What is bad about the essay?
What is the essence of the essay?
What would you do differently to make this an App-Kicking essay?
Other comments:

Final Draft AN- admitted ED to Duke

There is something about standing in a room full of wheelchair bound children to that will change a person. In that room Duchenne, Becker, and Emery-Dreifuss are not kids' names, but names of the monstrous neuromuscular diseases that prey upon the kids' physical, intellectual and emotional beings until there is nothing left to take. This was the room where I was introduced to the child who, in 6 short days, would change my life.

Before I had arrived at MDA Camp, a place where kids with muscular dystrophy can live unlimited uninhibited lives for one week a year and venture away from their ordinarily sheltered lives, I imagined it would be like any other volunteer work I did had done with helping kids. I had learned responsibility at Embry-Riddle Basketball Camps where I worked with "normal" kids and had spent countless hours patiently sharing the game I love with hyperactive nine year olds. I personified empathy from the time I had spent with the kids at the Remar orphanage in El Salvador. The smiles a simple hug could elicit or the giggles from a shared prank made it easy to genuinely love those kids.

So I thought I was ready, a patient, responsible, compassionate guy with a serving heart... I thought the week would be a breeze. However, as I sat and was introduced to my camper, Tristan, and gained a little brother for the week, I realized that it was going to be one of the most demanding weeks of my life.

Throughout that week I became Tristan's arms and legs. I found myself, constantly being humbled by the magnitude of my responsibilities. Having to treat a 9-year-old boy like a baby was an incredibly humbling experience that put my life into perspective. Every morning, I changed Tristan into his clothes while he sat there helpless. Whenever he needed to go to the bathroom I was right by his side to put him on the toilet and clean him when he was finished. At night, I was there to shower him and finally lift him into his bed as he began to drift off to sleep. I couldn't fathom what being totally exposed to a stranger, stripped of your pride and dignity, would be like. While it was hard for both of us, Tristan and I found strength within each other, and it was his smile that never failed to remind me of my purpose. I was at that camp to give Tristan the greatest week of his year; one he would never forget. It reminded me of the smiles on the kids' faces at the orphanage when they saw me each year when I returned or on the faces of the kids at basketball camp who were thrilled to start a week of camp. It was Tristan's never-ending smile that reminded me of the true potential I have to use my life to make change in this world, like I did in those kids' lives.

In life, there is no one experience that makes you an adult, but rather there are events and people that form the foundation of who you are in adulthood. While the basketball camps and mission trips were incredible experiences that I would never change for the world, the bond I formed with Tristan is going to be something that I will always draw strength from. Before I left for camp, my mom told me that I was going to be a blessing to my camper, which I believe I was, but I never could have imagined how much of a blessing Tristan was to me. Without Tristan I wouldn't be the a composed and mature young man striving to make a positive impact on the world and the people in it.

The road Tristan is on is a short and rough one, but I will be there with him every step of the way. I'll visit him often and make sure the final years of his life will be his best. No matter what, I find comfort in the fact that wherever life takes me he will be there with me, continually inspiring me to change the world one smile at a time.

Sample 3:

Original Essay EG

Prompt: *Common App - Some students have a background, identity, interest, or talent that is so meaningful they believe their application would be incomplete without it. If this sounds like you, then please share your story.*

I could feel my heart thumping in my chest. The curtain whooshed open and the breeze cooled my profusely sweating body. The crowd of cheering people suddenly erupted in laughter, and I feared for the worst as I mustered to speak. "How's it going?" I yelled into the microphone as my inner Adam Levine whispered into my ear, "is that the best you could do?" I was met with even louder and warmer applause as the jitters and the sweat completely evaporated. I looked at my band mates, remembered to breath, and gave the count.

Pivotal moments pop up out of nowhere like dry lightning, and like dry lightning, my five minutes of fame ignited a fire inside me. Suddenly, my life was divided into two parts. There was Ethan before the gong show, and Ethan after the gong show

Only two weeks earlier our motley crew had decided to rise out of our comfortable obscurity and enter the gong show. At first I was excited to play hoping that some of the ladies would notice my guitar playing talent, that was until I discovered that I had been signed up to sing. Although my live concerts put on for my soap and towel have always received widespread adoration, the idea of singing in front of over 400 people was terrifying. Now I had to overcome my fear of being in front of so many people, and unlike the cliché movie, I did not have an excellent voice hidden inside me. In fact, at my kindergarten school play, I was given the only speaking role. For two weeks, I practiced all the time. I rock and rolled all night, and part of the day, in the hopes of sounding adequate.

But those feelings of self-doubt belong to the old Ethan. The gong show unhooked the final latch inside me that enabled who I truly am to escape. A young, dashing, man, who possessed the confidence to truly make a difference replaced a boy who was scared to stand up for his beliefs. After the gong show, I realized it was my time to take ion. I pushed passed my doubts and fears of possible embarrassment, and put myself out there by running for and winning the position of NHS president. I stood up for my ideals, and presented my bill for Youth in Government in front of the entire House of Representatives. I wanted to be heard, and was chosen as a master of ceremonies for the Senior Awards at my school, an event which draws a crowd of over 1,000 people. Most importantly however, when I looked in the mirror, I didn't judge all the things that could be fixed, but instead I focused on the things that worked, and how I could improve them.

An hour before the start of the show, I was cramped in the back of the musty auditorium nervously pacing back and forth. Suddenly, a Target bag landed in my arms. "We are having a wardrobe change." My band mate said to me as I looked inside the bag. My stomach churned as I pulled out the bright red, ultra, short shorts and the youth-small, white t-shirt. I put on the outfit, and proceeded to waddle for the rest of the show, hoping to avoid an infamous wardrobe malfunction. As the curtains opened, we were met with surprisingly supportive applause.

Now, a year later, when I watch the YouTube video of our performance, I am struck by how little I moved, because inside I was Mick Jagger rocking the house down. My true passion is to one day run a business of my own, so there will likely be a lot more crowd sourcing than crowd surfing in my future. But this pivotal moment, albeit a small high school talent show, has given me the confidence to reach for my goals and truly believe that I will succeed.

Your feedback

What is good about the essay?
What is bad about the essay?
What is the essence of the essay?
What would you do differently to make this an App-Kicking essay?
Other comments:

Final Draft EG- admitted Duke ED

"Every New Beginning Comes from Some Other Beginning's End"

"How's it going?" I attempted to shout, but instead mumbled into the microphone. My inner Adam Levine whispered, "Is that the best you could do?"

Only two weeks earlier, our motley crew decided to rise out of our comfortable anonymity and enter the school Gong Show. With unforeseen consequences, I was assigned the role of lead vocalist in a unanimous vote that did not include me, despite my eight years of guitar experience and utter lack of vocal talent. I took many long showers, belting out tunes trying to smooth the cracks out of my voice. Although my shampoo bottle and showerhead became huge fans, I still feared that my pitch was far from perfect. There would be more than four hundred people in attendance, many of whom I would see regularly in my classes. This would be social suicide.

When the day finally arrived, I felt like I was a stranger in my own body. We were crammed behind the stage of the musty auditorium like a herd of cattle waiting for slaughter. Suddenly, a Target bag connected with my face, as one of my band mates shouted, "New wardrobe!" After squeezing into the extra small, youth white t-shirt and bright red short shorts, stretched past max capacity, I tried to calm myself down as my whole body began to shake. The curtains opened to an eruption of laughter and applause.

The bright spotlight masked the faces of the booming crowd and the fear within my heart. My jitters and sweat completely evaporated. I looked at my band mates, remembered to breathe, and gave the count. As the lyrics left my mouth, I could feel the fear and anxiety exit my body. The large auditorium transformed into my shower, and the microphone became my shampoo bottle. As the final notes echoed through the auditorium, the crowd cheered and the self-doubt that had plagued me for years was replaced with burgeoning confidence.

If my life was a band, what happened next was equivalent to worldwide fame. In February, I went to Youth in Government. I created a bill to provide healthy substitutes in vending machines and actively pushed my bill past screening committees to the House of Representatives. I was later chosen to represent my school at Boys State. Along with learning about the history of Florida, I was able to further my knowledge of government functioning and was elected to be a member of the House of Representatives.

Back at school, I debuted my sophomore album and ran for NHS president. Once elected, I led with confidence and began establishing programs. For example, I developed a system where students could sign up weekly to volunteer at one of the local food banks or soup kitchens in my area.

But all of these accomplishments were about me. I realized that I had to do more. After all, an artist performs for his or her fans, and now I had to perform for my community.

I was upset with the large-scale development in my area. Acres of thriving ecosystem were being replaced by all-you-can-eat buffets and strip malls. I began researching how to measure these negative externalities, which lead me to Duke professors Xiaboi Sung and Christopher Timmins. With their insight, I analyzed all of the properties in Volusia County to find the percentage of development in each city. From there, I created heat maps to illustrate development and presented my project to the Volusia County Economic committee.

The Gong Show was the metronome that put my life on track. Although I looked like Frankenstein in beachwear up on stage, in my mind I am was Steven Tyler commanding the stage. There will likely be more crowd sourcing than crowd surfing in my future, but until then, all the world's a stage, so why not be a rock star?

Sample 4:

Original Draft MT

Prompt: *Common App- Some students have a background, identity, interest, or talent that is so meaningful they believe their application would be incomplete without it. If this sounds like you, then please share your story.*

After almost a month she finally comes to life. My 1972 Yamaha gives a few quick spurts and I quickly reach for the throttle. I give her some more gas and she starts her usual loud roar filled with backfires. I throw up the kickstand and I go for a ride before she inevitably dies out. I cruise through my neighborhood, trying to keep quiet, hoping the neighbors will not be annoyed. She's running pretty well considering this is the first time she's been driven in awhile. I get around the first corner on my street and accelerate quickly out of it. I gently squeeze the brakes to slow back down. I hear a harsh skidding and find myself losing control of my motorcycle. Before the halfway point of my ride, I was on the ground with the bike on top of me. I do my usual routine, get out from under the bike, check out my injuries, and then pull the bike back up. After years of experience my 450 pound Yamaha becomes easy to pull up. I put her on her kickstand and find the source of my crash, a seized front brake. I take the brake apart in the middle of the street and wheel the bike home.

Fixing things has become second nature. I dedicate some my knowledge of fixing things to my father, but most of it to the internet. I have come a long way and have learned a lot since I have been a child. As a child I constantly broke things, mostly myself. I was notorious for always hurting myself. I cracked my head open twice on the same place, after that my mother forced me to wear a helmet. I would always get cut by oysters and had a few hospital visits for the more severe cuts. Before I had a motorcycle I loved to ride my bike as fast as I could on and off the streets. My bike was responsible for more cuts and bruises than I can count. The story my parents will never let me forget is the time I broke my foot from holding onto my garage door and riding it to the top.

The start of my musical interests became the end of my bodily injuries. I started playing drums in the fourth grade and I was hooked from there. I loved to play by myself but quickly learned that I preferred to play in a band. I played with my local church and soon went to high school and joined the band program. It was in high school that I fell in love with not just drums but music as a whole. Music has presented me with so many unique opportunities to share my passion and perform to others. Now looking back it makes sense that my parents would support my musical interests so that I would stop doing things that would result in injuring myself. I see that my parents tried to shift my focus to safer means of entertainment.

After wheeling my motorcycle back into the garage, I notice the small accident had little created little damage. Some small scrapes on the exhaust, a broken turn signal, and a broken brake lever, nothing hard to fix. I get right to work repairing the front brake, thinking of that rewarding feeling I will get when the motorcycle will be up to driving condition again. I have always found interest working with my hands. Whether it is repairing a car, motorcycle, or simply working around the house, finding things that need to be fixed. When I work with my hands my mind can wonder and work seems to go by faster. My favorite part of repairing things is the feeling of satisfaction I get when the item is fixed and operational.

What is good about the essay?
What is bad about the essay?
What is the essence of the essay?
What would you do differently to make this an App-Kicking essay?
Other comments:

Final Draft MT- admitted EA University of Miami

The two short rumbles are music to my ears after an hour of kicking. They catch me by surprise, and I take a moment to catch my breath. I have successfully rebuilt my first motorcycle. I jump on the kick starter and hear a low grumble, giving the throttle more gas until I hear a beautiful roar and a few backfires. After months in the grave, my 1972 Yamaha has finally risen from the ashes. Cruising through my neighborhood, I try to contain myself and not ride too loudly. My excitement, however, exceeds my caution and I open up the throttle. The houses flying by remind me to slow down, so I gently squeeze the brakes. Instead of a welcomed deceleration, I hear a harsh skidding and lose my balance. Before the halfway point of my ride, I am on the ground with the bike on top of me. I drag myself from under the bike, check out my injuries, and then pull up the bike. After years of experience, my 450 pound Yamaha has become easy to lift. I throw her up on her kickstand and find the cause of my crash, a seized front brake. I whip out my tool kit and deftly dismantle the broken part.

Fixing things has become second nature to me. I attribute some of my mechanical knowledge to the genetic contributions of my father, but most of it I owe to a higher power: the internet. I have come a long way from my clumsy childhood, when I was notorious for self-induced bodily injuries. Growing up near the beach, I always got cut by oysters while wading in the water and had a few hospital visits to stitch the more severe lacerations. On land, I cracked my head open twice in the same place, and after that my mother forced me to wear a helmet around. Before I had a motorcycle I loved to ride my bike as fast as I could on and off the streets. That bike was responsible for more cuts and bruises than I can count. My worst injury, however, was breaking my foot after riding my electric garage door. That injury and my resulting immobility, marked a turning point in my life.

The start of my musical interest coincided with the end of my bodily injuries. Maybe that is why my parents cultivated it so fervently. Without knowing it, I found a love for rhythm from my brother tapping on my helmet with sticks to annoy me. The first time I was able to play on a real drum set I was hooked. I liked playing loudly and having the freedom to improvise. My drums provided a great physical outlet, and any practice session was better than the gym. As much as I enjoy playing alone, I prefer to jam with other musicians. The music program at my high school has offered me incredible performance opportunities and has taught me a lot about life on a more expansive stage. Traveling to play in London, and competing in the Savannah Swing Central Jazz Competition, have allowed me to test my skills and share my passion for music with larger audiences.

Dripping in sweat and feeling like I just finished a three hour jam session, I manage to wheel the motorcycle home. The accident didn't cause much damage, nothing hard to fix. I get to work making repairs, craving that feeling of accomplishment I get when my project is finished. Crashing my bike or messing up a song by missing a beat are small problems to mend. I realize that the world today is complicated, and risky, but working with my hands allows me to contemplate the problems I can solve. Amongst the world's loud and imperfect rhythms, there will be challenges to face. I want to continue to find creative solutions. Even if I break my hands, I'm ready to play.

Sample 5:

Original Draft MH

Prompt: *Common app Recount an incident or time when you experienced failure. How did it affect you, and what lessons did you learn?*

Crouched under the shade of the weeping willow by the lake in the backyard, I was bawling. 7-year old me was devastated and helpless, fearing the worst: Are they going to die?

I gaped in horror as I watched their scales abruptly blacken and peel. After stage 1, shock, and stage 2, panic, I decided upon a course of action. With much care, like a doctor to a wounded patient, I set each of them down gently in the soft, damp soil of my potted tomato plant. A cold water rinse, regular check-ups and TLC were what I prescribed for treatment in an attempt to right my wrongs.

That summer's afternoon, as per usual, I was barefoot outside satisfying my curiosity when I was struck with a brilliant idea. It began as a spa day, courtesy of yours truly. I took care to fill a glass dish with lukewarm water, shells and stones to perch on, and fresh, pink rose petals, the finishing touch of luxury. Who was I pampering? Lizards.

While other kids were catching waves, colds, and falling stars (to put into their pockets), I was catching lizards and unintentionally performing science experiments. Long before I knew it existed, I was using the scientific method to find out more about the world I live in.

What is good about the essay?

What is bad about the essay?

What is the essence of the essay?

What would you do differently to make this an App-Kicking essay?

Other comments:

Final draft MH - accepted to Dartmouth off the waitlist

I was devastated. Helpless. Crouched under the shade of the weeping willow by the lake in the backyard, I was sobbing. 7-year old me feared the worst: Are they going to die? I gaped in horror as I watched their scales abruptly blacken and peel before my eyes. After stage 1, shock, and stage 2, panic, I had to take action. Like a doctor tending to a wounded patient, I set them down gently in the soft, damp soil of my potted tomato plant. A cold-water rinse, regular check-ups and TLC were what I prescribed for treatment in an attempt to right my egregious mistake.

That summer's afternoon, I was barefoot outside, as usual satisfying my curiosity when I got a brilliant idea. It would be a spa day! I carefully filled a glass dish with lukewarm water, shells and stones to perch on, and fresh, pink rose petals- the finishing touch of luxury. Who exactly was the pampering for? No, not my deserving mom like it should have been- it was for lizards, of course!

While other kids were catching waves, balls, and falling stars (to put into their pockets), I was catching Brown Anoles. Long before I knew it existed, I was using the scientific method to discover the world for myself. My curious nature made me wonder what would happen if I grew a plant on the side of the house with an abundance of sunlight versus the side with less sun; what if I threw this type of rock into the lake- would it skip? At an early age, I realized everything was an opportunity to learn something new. Despite the popularity of Playstation 2s and GameCubes, I was (and still am) one of those kids who loved to go out and explore, who genuinely appreciated and enjoyed learning for fun. Yes, I was a budding scientist with an inquiring mind and an eagerness to understand- I intuitively made observations and was more than happy to "test my hypotheses."

Our experiences are the results of life's experiments; we can learn from the outcomes. When I realized this, I felt unstoppable. I had the power to achieve different results just by changing some aspects of an experiment. Good, bad or undesirable, what you learn from all results is invaluable. For instance, I learned that if you use Palmolive dish soap to wash lizards, then their skin will dry and blacken (but they will recover with a little rest) because lizards don't need baths. I learned that the shower has the absolute best acoustics for those high Cs in an Italian aria. Also through trial and error, I learned that taking three IB science courses in one year is crazy but not unmanageable; that wishing people 'Happy Earth Day!' is an effective icebreaker and means of campaigning for Student Government – I could continue, but I have also learned through 'experim-ence' that attention spans are short and that your interest is crucial.

Although these little life experiments may seem trivial at times, they have helped to develop and nurture my inquisitive nature. Now I perform these life experiments on a daily basis without realizing it.

I hope to be part of a team that can help our society and our earth through biological sciences. I plan on using scientific experiments in my research; after all I've had over a decade of experimenting experience already. I've set this very essay up as an experiment as well: I hypothesize a favorable outcome- the conclusion is for **you** to write.

8.4 How do you make a good essay great?

Which of the essays above resonated most with you and why?

As you reflect on the essay samples above and the transformations they went through, consider how they became better. One of the key aspects is to do more with your essay. Tie together some different components of your life, but always remember that the essay is not a place to list everything you have accomplished. Take a unique approach: In Sample 5, you could see how the student tied in her love of science, and in Sample 4 you could see the same thing done with music instead. These applicants are clearly different, but both of their essays present engaging stories.

Ultimately, that is the key: writing an engaging story. Draw your reader in, make them *feel* something. But writing a great essay takes more than that. We have read first drafts that had us in tears yet still took a dozen revision drafts to perfect. Always remember this: **there is nothing more important that you will write this year, perhaps even in all of high school, than this essay**. Don't worry about every little detail at first; find the essence of it. But then fine tune the essay- sentence by sentence, word by word, until your message comes through clearly.

When in doubt, try to elevate your writing. In simple terms, this means to make it better and reach the next level. Like trying to beat a better team in a game or outperform a more experienced dancer or performer, you will need to take your writing game to the next level, depending on the colleges you are applying to.

8.5 Making a clean break

There is a point in the essay-writing process where you might need to consider the possibility of going a different direction. This brings us back to the reason it is so important to take time to think of a strong topic and thoroughly outline the essay. Even so, sometimes your current draft just isn't going anywhere. Sometimes it is hard to let go after you have put so much time and effort into it, but you need to be clinical about it. If the essay fizzles, if you can't elevate it, if you just aren't feeling it anymore, then at the very least it is probably time to set it aside and work on something else. Maybe that something else is a supplemental essay, or resume work- but maybe it should be taking a shot at an essay with an entirely different topic or a different approach with your current topic. Whatever the case, remember that you want to make a choice you won't regret. It is certainly a bummer to toss something you have worked hard on, but if it won't give you a good chance of admission then it is better to move on now than to regret not moving on if you get a rejection letter a few months later.

8. Concluding thoughts

The essay is the core of the application, the place to make your case for admission to the school. Remember that when you apply to appropriately challenging schools (those for which you test scores and grades would make you a qualified applicant), your story is what will put you over the top. Everyone you are competing with will likely have those same grades and scores- so the essay is what can really set you apart. While you work on the essays and edit to perfection, keep in mind that every word matters and every bit of extra work (or sleep lost because of that work) will be worth it in the long run.

8. Action Items

- ❏ Start generating topics early; you will likely write many essays, so the more topics you generate, the better
- ❏ Avoid jumping right into a draft, outline and free write first instead to establish good content before putting the constraints of grammatical conventions into place
- ❏ Edit to perfection. When you are done editing, edit some more
- ❏ Good writing begets good writing: the more you write, the better you will get at it so start early on your essay writing and work tirelessly retooling your essays

Chapter 9:

Supplemental Essays

9.1 Supplemental essays and materials

Since your application needs to speak for itself, you should view the supplemental essays as another opportunity to showcase your qualifications to the school. This process is often specifically aligned to the school you are applying to, so it will help you connect to the school. The most important factor in creating effective supplemental essays is understanding why you want to apply to the school you are applying to. As you begin to consider topics for the supplementals, remember that the more that your application is centrally focused around your story, the more you will come off the screen to them. **Kicking Apps** means that your supplementals should add to your story- not distract the reader from it.

The best way to be sure that this happens is to plan in advance. Weave together your collection of activities that you are involved in into a centralized story. Perhaps, without knowing it, you actually had a focus all along; perhaps the story was growing organically from your interests. Or maybe you have a disjointed collection of clubs and sports and community service all just done to have fodder for a resume. What then? Now is the time to find the common thread among them. And there may still be some time to add in a few other elements during senior year to make it all come together.

9.2 The Why (____) essay

Almost every school with supplemental essays asks some version of the question "Why us?" This is where you show the college that you understand what it offers and why you would fit well there. Remember, though, that they already know everything about themselves. You are still mostly conveying information about yourself- not about them. So this is the time to tell a story that uniquely connects you to what that specific university seeks to accomplish.

Let's face it: A top school doesn't want you to apply there just because it is prestigious. They want you to apply because there is some unique aspect of the college's specific culture that you know you can contribute to. Again, remember that any topic will work for any essay; your artful twist on it is the way to earn recognition.

Why this school in particular

College	
Relevant Aspects of the school	Your story that connects to them

College	
Relevant Aspects of the school	Your story that connects to them

College	
Relevant Aspects of the school	Your story that connects to them

9.3 Topic selection for your Supplementals

If you have multiple schools that require supplemental essays, especially schools that give you a choice of essays to answer, you should to lay them all out together to look for overlap between topics. Just doing one college's supplements at a time is ineffective and inefficient. Once you see all of the topics, we recommend that you highlight the ones that have similarities. For example, every essay that asks you to expand on an activity for 150 words should be highlighted with orange. Once you see the overlap, go back to your topic brainstorm and find the topic(s) that work best for each one.

Then go through the full essay writing process for each one and start revising. As one essay starts to take shape, get another one started and continue in this way- instead of editing one all the way to completion before starting the next. We call this process the essay writing spiral: as an essay comes together take a break from it to start another, move those two along then start the next and so on. As you complete some essays they exit the spiral and others enter to take their place

Supplement topic organizing matrix

College	Prompt	Content/topic

9.4 Some examples of Supplements

Supplemental essays are not just an afterthought; they are a critical component of a successful application. You should devote as much time, effort, and planning to them as you would do for your main essay. Remember that they should also showcase you as a strong applicant, not just be a loose collection of ideas. IF AN ADMISSIONS COUNCELOR READS A POOR QUALITY SUPPLEMENT FOR THEIR SCHOOL AFTER A HIGH QUALITY MAIN ESSAY THEY ASSUME THAT YOU ARE NOT REALLY SERIOUS ABOUT THEIR SPECIFIC SCHOOL AND ITS APPLICATION,

As you look at the essays below, again consider the message that the writer is attempting to convey and how he or she showcases their identity to the admissions counselors.

Sample 1:

Prompt: *Duke University Seeks A Talented, Engaged Student Body That Embodies The Wide Range Of Human Experience; We Believe That The Diversity Of Our Students Makes Our Community Stronger. If You'd Like To Share A Perspective You Bring Or Experiences You've Had To Help Us Understand You Better – Perhaps Related To A Community You Belong To, Your Sexual Orientation Or Gender Identity, Or Your Family Or Cultural Background – We Encourage You To Do So. Real People Are Reading Your Application, And We Want To Do Our Best To Understand And Appreciate The Real People Applying To Duke. (250 Words Maximum)*

Final draft EG - admitted Duke early decision

My daily classroom bell is the familiar whine of a Cessna engine. I live in the largest fly-in community in the world. Our playground is a 4000' runway connected to our homes by winding taxiways. This school specializes in living history, and I'm late for class.

I rush to Dr. Jerry Berlin's class to talk to him about teambuilding for my upcoming group project. A world-renowned psychologist, he developed cockpit resource management, empowering co-pilots in the cockpit, creating a horizontal team dynamic.

With prospects of success on the project I headed for my lesson on literary devices. Today, it is irony with Cpt. Yellin, a WWII fighter pilot with PTSD. He faced emotional turmoil when his son married the daughter of a Japanese fighter pilot. These men, mortal enemies forty years prior, were now connected through love.

Continuing to ponder the enduring power of love I head to Women's Studies. A British Navy and commercial pilot, Kate Burrows was rescued from the Irish Sea after losing both engines. A fearless aviator and role model, today she reminds me of the necessity of me preparedness, and overcoming challenges despite adversity.

These de facto teachers have helped me file the flight plan for my future. Even after six years, I am continually amazed by the interesting people I add to my logbook. My community reflects the importance of a mentally stimulating environment. The Duke community is a place where I can stretch my mind and my intellectual curiosity can take flight.

Sample 2:

Prompt: *Elaborate on one of your extracurricular activities (150 word).*

Final Draft CN - admitted Tulane regular decision

The youngest sailor to circumnavigate the globe was a 16-year-old Dutch girl. While I didn't match her feat I tasted the courage she personified. As day faded into night off the Greek island of Hydra, the sky was a canvas plastered with magnificent blues and oranges. My sister and I were anchored aboard our 50ft catamaran anxiously awaiting our parents return from their evening row. Summoning all of my courage in the gathering darkness, I hauled up the anchor and piloted out of the safe harbor into rough seas in search of them. My nerves were assuaged when I found them, worn out and adrift with a broken oar. In that pivotal moment I didn't wait for an outcome but instead charted my own course. As I sail into my future I will not be deterred by unfavorable winds but will instead push my craft towards the limitless horizon.

Sample 3

Prompt: *In 2017, Transcending Boundaries will be a defining theme at Wake Forest. What boundaries have played a role in shaping the individual you are today? How will you engage the Wake Forest community to expand your view of the world?*

Final Draft SS - Wake Forest regular decision

Death of a Lawyer

Lieutenant Horatio Caine, CSI Miami's top cop, arrives at a murder scene in his black SUV, dramatically puts on his sunglasses, and coolly says to reporters, "This case is unprecedented – there is a victim but no body!" The Police Department's Crime Scene Investigators scrutinize the scene. The deceased in this case is rather unusual; it is my destiny to become a lawyer. My parents, late grandfather, uncles, great uncles and cousins are all lawyers. My brother dreams of following in my family's footsteps; I, on the other hand, want to follow a different path.

I have called upon the renowned Lieutenant Caine and Calleigh Duquesne, his best CSI, to find out why I do not fit the traditional Stack family mold of natural born lawyers. Growing up, I was obsessed with Nate the Great books, and later, the well-loved Nancy Drew mysteries. As I grew older, my interest in mysteries gravitated towards the criminal justice system. I was intrigued with the process used by forensic scientists to solve crimes. In particular, I followed the career path of Lieutenant Caine, never missing an episode, as he and his team labored to achieve justice for unfortunate souls with untimely endings.

Alexx Woods, the CSI Medical Examiner, meticulously surveys the crime scene to ascertain the cause of this crime. Known for conversing with cadavers to discover the cause of their fate, she mumbles, "The lawyer glove simply didn't fit." Woods' investigation uncovers a multitude of grisly facts. As a child, I tormented my brother with my love of vaccinations, knowing he was deathly afraid of them! I was intrigued with different facets of the medical field, including looking at x-rays of stomachs with coins, knives and other objects within them. The sight of blood never bothered me. I eagerly shadowed our family veterinarian as he performed animal surgeries and treated dogs and cats in his office; I also met with an FBI agent to learn about Quantico. Much to my family's surprise, I gravitated towards math and science, rather than public speaking and politics, and my eyes glazed over during family legal discussions. Then during a summer medical institute, I sutured chicken legs and dissected a rat.

Chemistry and Forensic Science were my favorite classes in high school and, in particular, I was fascinated with toxicology. Testing a suspect's tissue samples and bodily fluids to obtain justice for victims and bring closure for their families piqued my curiosity. I developed a newfound interest in one day possibly collecting, preserving and analyzing evidence, alongside a team like Lieutenant Caine's. I even imagined that one day, I might fill his shoes as the Director of the Miami-Dade Crime Lab!

In a strange twist, Lieutenant Caine interviewed a family member who confirmed his suspicion that this mysterious death was, in part, the result of an "inside job." Under relentless questioning, my grandma confessed to Lieutenant Caine that from the time I was born, she had consciously and stealthily endeavored to steer me in a direction other than law. Thus, she seized upon every birthday and holiday season to inundate me with scientific and medical books and games, including Operation and Clue, to spark my interest in these fields. Grandma sighed, "There were simply too many lawyers in our family!"

Based upon their review of the indisputable evidence, Lieutenant Caine and his team put to rest once and for all the foregone conclusion that I am destined to become a lawyer. Instead, they unequivocally concluded that it is more likely that my future career path is veering towards the uncharted waters of science or medicine. My family stoically accepts this conclusion and somberly buries the pre-made sign which reads, Stack, Stack & Stack.

Sample 4:

Prompt: *Duke University Seeks A Talented, Engaged Student Body That Embodies The Wide Range Of Human Experience; We Believe That The Diversity Of Our Students Makes Our Community Stronger. If You'd Like To Share A Perspective You Bring Or Experiences You've Had To Help Us Understand You Better – Perhaps Related To A Community You Belong To, Your Sexual Orientation Or Gender Identity, Or Your Family Or Cultural Background – We Encourage You To Do So. Real People Are Reading Your Application, And We Want To Do Our Best To Understand And Appreciate The Real People Applying To Duke. (250 Words Maximum)*

Final draft AN - Duke admitted early decision

I may not have been raised by wolves, but growing up I was always part of a pack of dogs. Brown, black, yellow, white, three-legged, blind, young, old, labs, retrievers; any variety you can imagine has been raised in my house. Dog after dog came to us needing comfort and love and sometimes a little bit more. They all had different backgrounds, but each one became part of my story, "A Day In the Life of a Lab Rescue Foster Parent."

As a young boy attending a small private school I grew accustomed to the homogeneity in the world – we all had similar backgrounds, belief systems, and ethnicities. When I entered public school I was thrust into a world of diversity. While some of my peers were paralyzed by this change, I thrived in my newfound world of variety. I owe my seamless transition to my K9 housemates.

You see it didn't matter what background each of my furry, rescued friends came from. They all had different personalities and tendencies, but at their core they all had an underlying need to be loved, accepted, and feel valued. Sounds familiar doesn't it?

I look forward to continuing to explore the world's diversity through my college experience. As part of the Duke community, I will seek opportunities to learn from the diverse perspectives of my peers and have my own personal impact on Duke life. Together, immersed in the Duke culture that fosters champions, we will work to make the world a better place.

Sample 5:

Prompt: *For applicants to Columbia College, please tell us what from your current and past experiences (either academic or personal) attracts you specifically to the field or fields of study that you noted in the Member Questions section. If you are currently undecided, please write about any field or fields in which you may have an interest at this time. (300 words or less)*

Final draft DH - Emory admitted regular decision

At five years old, I listened attentively to the boisterous political discussions that filled my household regarding the presidential election. My parents have always encouraged me to be active in the political system, and they were never shy about their views. As a result, neither am I. I was the only kid in elementary school to know the difference between a Republican and a Democrat, and the only kid to bear a strong political opinion.

When the 2008 election season began, I was old enough to truly participate. My parents created an environment conducive to discussion and learning. We followed every debate and news story of President Obama's historic campaign, and I offered a pointed opinion of each event in the election process. This is when I discovered my passion for politics, and particularly my passion for equality. From then on, I made it my personal mission to educate my friends and freely offer them a scathing glare if they claimed "not to care about politics." When a classmate or acquaintance begins a political discussion, it is as if a fire is ignited within me. After taking the AP Human Geography course with "Human Johnson," one of the greatest teachers to live on this earth, I knew that I had to dedicate my life to studying the ways of the world and the ways of improving human life (and I of course had to run for president in 2036).

I know that this all begins with an exploration of government, the structure of society. This year's Presidential election has led me to solidify my career path. Being old enough to be taken at least semi-seriously, I have been able to convert my beliefs into action, starting a local Young Democrats chapter, volunteering in campaign affairs, and debating with my peers.

Analysis of the supplements

Sample	Essence of the essay	Who is this applicant?
1		
2		
3		
4		
5		

Which of the essays resonated most with you and why?

9. **Concluding Thoughts**

One of the biggest mistakes you can make is to treat supplemental essays as an afterthought because you think they won't make a difference. Always remember that they are indeed part of the application, so they most certainly make a difference. The supplementals allow you to complete your story. They bring even more depth and authenticity to you as a person, helping you come further off the screen for the reader and become more memorable. At the very least, the level of writing in your supplements must be equal to your main essay. Put your heart into each and every aspect of your application and build an irrefutable case for acceptance.

9. Action items

- ❏ Find all of your topics for your supplemental essays
- ❏ Identify those that will cross over partially or completely to save yourself some work
- ❏ Select topics for each of the supplementals
- ❏ Follow the same process you completed for writing your main essay

Chapter 10:

Additional essay concerns

10.1 Some final thoughts on essays.

Whatever you do with your essays and your entire application, you need to keep in mind the same guiding question: How is this going to convince the school to admit me instead of another applicant? Writing something powerful but offensive probably isn't the best approach. The old myth about the kid who wrote the essay for Harvard about taking risks and simply wrote in crayon on the paper, "This is taking a risk," probably isn't true- but it speaks to the breadth of possibility in the application process. (Granted, since most applications are all electronic, the crayon's power has kind of been diminished anyway but you still have options to consider.)

10.2 What's in a name?

"Should my essay have a title?" While not every essay needs a title, an effective one can set the stage very well for the reader and frame the whole perception of the essay. A title should only be used if it is a contributing factor, if it adds something to your essay; if not, then like anything else it has no real place in your essay. Note how sample 3 in chapter 8 used an effective title.

One good option for a title is to take it from the conclusion sentence. Another is a use a catchy salient point from the essay. You will notice a few samples in the previous chapters and on our app kicking website that use titles and others that do not. This is a personal and a case-by-case decision: if you title one of your essays for a particular school you still don't necessarily need to title all of them. It is something you should definitely consider and if it adds to your story then by all means include one.

10.3 Taking a risk

Your goal on the essay is to make yourself memorable, likable, and ultimately a candidate who they want to admit to their school. How you do that may involve taking some risks. One such risk is the use of profanity. Depending on your essay and your audience, it could help or hurt you tremendously. Another risk is to write about topics that may cast you in a negative light: eating disorders, cheating, substance abuse, etc. The key is not the suitability of the topics themselves but rather how they are used. Writing about having an eating disorder would not necessarily make a strong essay, but writing about overcoming an eating disorder and the positive self-growth that resulted from it would.

Case study of RA

When we began working with RA on his quest for admission to Stanford, he was a sophomore. After much discussion and planning, we decided to help him paint his personal portrait as a scholar-athlete who demonstrated academic superiority and leadership within the school and community.

RA took care of his athletics, quickly becoming a top receiver on his school's football team and a track star. We worked together to improve his test scores, and he earned a 34 on the ACT®. In school, he was the valedictorian. With a leadership position in student government and in a foundation that helped sick children in the community, he was a compelling applicant. Still, his application needed something more to put it over the top.

As he planned and worked on essays he sought out ways to shine. His main essay available on our app kicking website (www.kickingapps.org) focused on his hands: how they were ugly but helped him to catch footballs, play the piano, and serve the community. In a unique way, he showed his depth but he really distinguished himself in the supplemental essays. One of them (below) addressed a potentially controversial topic. In the end, he was admitted to his dream school and now attends Stanford.

Sample:

Prompt: *Stanford students possess an intellectual vitality. Reflect on an idea or experience that has been important to your intellectual development. (100 to 250 words)*

Final draft RA - admitted to Stanford early decision

The summer before my junior year, I was in a situation that prompted immediate action: in order to enroll in Calculus BC my senior year, I had to complete the entire online Pre-Calculus curriculum in just two months.

Churning out two, three, or sometimes even four lessons a day from the comfort of Starbucks, everything was going great until I completed module six of ten and realized that I could not take the exam for it: my teacher was on vacation and unable to give me the exam password. After failed attempts to contact her and even the department head, I knew I only had one recourse: I had to hack into the exam.

After cracking the code for the module six exam, I soon found myself using the same cipher (names of fruits) to hack into the modules seven, eight, nine and ten exams, finishing the entire second semester before my teacher returned. With this pace, I completed the entire course with an A average and a few weeks to spare.

Like the proverbial apple that hit Newton's head, this experience catalyzed a rapid spike in the level of my academic inquiry: I now try to fill every gap of time in my day with opportunities to further expand my knowledge, whether that be by working on an AP Bio class online or learning how to speak Spanish through CD's played in my car.

So this student essentially hacked into the exams for his online class, a potentially very off-putting topic for an admission counselor, but you can see from the way that he treated the subject he used it to his advantage.

10.4 Use of quotes

It is common practice for students to use a quote within their essay either as an introduction, a transition, or part of a strong conclusion. Quotes themselves are not going to make your essay better, but if the quote is relevant and powerful then it can certainly help to strengthen the story you are creating. Again this is a case by case judgment, not part of a magic formula.

10.5 Some final thoughts on topic selection

We return again to the idea of topic selection. Until you are done with all of your essays, topic selection should always be on your mind. Remember that any topic, with the right spin, can work for any prompt, but you should really think about what you are writing and how you are writing it throughout the whole process. So here are some reminders:

1. Be unique in the topics you address or the way you address them.

2. Do not write about sex, drugs or rock and roll (unless you do so in an incredibly compelling way).

3. Dig deep to determine the message that your topic conveys to the reader.

4. Make sure the topic matches the prompt, no matter how you write it.

10. Conclusion

When working on your essays, continually reevaluate what you are writing and how you are writing it. There are no "best tricks" that will help you. What you need to do instead of searching for the magic application bullet is really dig in on your own essays and find your best approach for you. That is ultimately going to provide you with your best chances of admission to the school of your choice.

10. Action Items

- ❏ Decide independently if each of your essays needs a title or not
- ❏ If you are working with a "risky" topic, consider whether you are making it work for you or against you
- ❏ Decide if you want to use a quote in your essay- and if so, make sure it adds to the essay and does not detract or distract from your central message
- ❏ When you think your app is done, look back at the little details and make sure you are comfortable with everything

Chapter 11:

Recommendation Letters

11.1 Rec Letters

We touched on recommendation letters earlier. In this section, we are going to talk about how to get **App Kicking** rec letters. Not all recommendations are created equal, and recs that really stand out resonate with admissions counselors. People reading your application will expect recommendations to be glowing and even somewhat over the top, so one that is flat or even bad can really stand out in a negative way. Other recommendation letters can sound like the kind your mother would write about you: boasting about what a wonderful, kind, smart, and hardworking individual you are, but without much substance. Imagine reading through literally thousands of rec letters; ones like these would either be completely forgotten by the evaluator- or worse make them feel like reading them was a waste of their time.

There are, in fact, some schools that do view rec letters as a waste of time and don't accept them (UF might even hold it against you if you send one for example). While you can't control every word that someone writes about you, you can control how teachers, coaches, bosses, and others view you and the amount of effort and emotion that they will put into a letter on your behalf.

11.2 How to stand out to your teachers ahead of time

You don't have to be a kiss up to get on the right side of teachers. (Remember success in this process is about app kicking not ass kissing). Step one is to do the basics: be attentive, polite, and respectful, and complete your assignments on time. Standing out, however, takes more than just being well behaved. You could help other students in your class who are struggling with the content, you could go the extra mile to participate in competitions or projects in the subject area, you could also elect to take advanced classes with the same teacher. Most teachers sponsor some kind of club; attend a meeting and if it interests you get involved and seek leadership positions in the club. Not only does this give you an opportunity to make a connection with your teacher, but you might be exposed to something the might spark a new passion for you. Sometimes this happens organically and sometimes you need a push – here are some options.

Ask questions: Not questions like "when is that due," but questions about current events in the field they teach or just current events in general. Ask questions after class or during your lunch. A great question to ask a teacher related to an assignment is, "How can I make this better?" (assuming of course that you put effort into it already).

Be positive: This is a good practice in general. People like to be around, work with, and help positive people. Nobody likes to have to endure pity parties all the time or feel like you only come around when you need help or have a problem. If you are somewhat cynical or sarcastic by nature, be careful not to overdo it.

Dig deeper: Is there a way for you to take the subject matter from a particular class to the next level of engagement? Try to enter the science fair, the social studies fair, a writing contest, or even the foreign language festival. Is there a related summer program or extracurricular activity you could join?

Show up for extra help: If the teacher offers review sessions or office hours show up with questions, participate, show that you value the subject and your grade in it. Nothing stands out like a student going the extra mile in a particular subject.

Offer to tutor: Peer tutoring can be very helpful to teachers and can help you personally gain a new degree of mastery in the subject. Volunteer to do this and show your commitment while polishing off your own skills in the process.

11.3 How to choose an App Kicking recommender

Ask teachers who know you well:

Be intentional about who you ask. Just because a teacher is popular or you like him or her does not mean he or she can write a good recommendation letter for you. Again, application evaluators expect recommendations to be glowing, so a bad one can be very detrimental. Here are some things to consider when asking for recommendation letters.

Is there a particular experience you had with the recommender that you want them to communicate?

What characteristics or personality traits do you want them to discuss about you?

Do they know you in a different context than your other recommenders? How do they know you differently?

Were their specific obstacles you overcame in their class?

Is a particular teacher known to write stellar letters? (Ask around, this is public knowledge if you dig for it).

Don't just ask teachers:

A teacher is generally going to approach the recommendation from an academic perspective. You want to get the admissions counselor to make a connection with you as a person as well as a student. The best way to do that is to give them a complete view of you including multiple perspectives. Think about people outside of school or in the school who know you outside the classroom. These would include coaches, pastors or other church members, immediate supervisors at work, Boy Scout/Girl Scout leaders, employees of charities you regularly volunteer for, and others.

Give them guidance on the content you want included:

Be intentional about who you ask and what you ask them to write about you. You want to make sure you have different references from your different recommenders. You would like to have at least one letter that addresses you as a student including your academic accolades, one that discusses your character as a person, and one that focuses on your level of involvement in your school and broader community. If you happen to have someone who can relate how you saved a baby panda from a burning building on your way to read to terminally ill children, that would work as well.

Make sure you give them plenty of time:

You want more than just a copy and pasted form-letter recommendation. You want one that reflects a part of you that is not already in your application. You want someone else's personal experience with you to come to life on the screen. That takes time to write, so give them plenty of it and let them know when the deadline is. A good guideline would be to request rec letters at least a month before they are due. If you can plan ahead and ask at the end of junior year you would give them all of summer break to work on your letter.

11.4 Use a Cover Letter to request recommendation

A letter requesting a recommendation from someone is an extremely effective tool to make sure you get the **App Kicking** rec letter you want. Most students will ask for a recommendation, give the potential recommender a form or request from the application site, and then just assume that it will get done. Even worse, some students just send an email invite without ever talking to recommender. Below is an example of a request for a recommendation letter that could be tailored to whomever you are asking. Be sure to hand them a copy of your resume with this letter so that they see you from a broader perspective as well.

Sample Letter to Request Recommendations for College Admissions

Date

Dear (address it to a specific individual)

I am writing to request that you write some college recommendation letters on my behalf. The letters and associated forms will be for the following schools.

List Schools you will be applying to (one per line) and include the location of the rec (paper, common ap, etc.) as well as the date you need it submitted by

The Common Application recommendations will be available to you through an email that the site will generate and send to you. I have also included the paper recommendations for you with addressed and stamped envelopes for those schools requiring that method. Please note the due dates for the letters listed above. If you would like me to mail the letters I will collect them from you once you have finished and sealed them.

I am applying to these schools with plans to study *(include details of your plans).* Based on my performance in your class I was hoping that you might comment specifically on my *(include the details you would like them to talk about and be sure to differentiate this between your different references).*

To help you complete these recommendations I have included a resume that details my accomplishments in your class and beyond. While in your class I also *(insert the highlights of your work in their class in particular in case they have forgotten* – grades, projects, outstanding contributions, aspects you learned from or liked the most).

If you have any questions please contact me by phone *(insert number)* or email *(insert address).* Thank you for taking your time to write these letters for me, I appreciate that you are very busy with your teaching schedule and am grateful that you have taken you time to help me in this way.

Sincerely

Your name

Your contact info

Notice that this letter not only gives all the information the recommender needs to submit the letter, but also gives them ideas about what you want them to include. You will more than likely never actually get to see any of your rec letters, but this will help you know who is writing what about you. Do not worry about this appearing overly forward or pretentious, a good recommender wants to write the best rec letter possible for you, this is just your way of helping to ensure that happens.

Additionally, you have listed for them (preferably in chronological order) what schools you are applying to and when their applications are due. You have made their job much easier by giving them something they can use as a reminder to get it done.

11.5 Follow up

After a few weeks, send a follow up email or pop in on your recommenders and make sure they have completed it. Most of the time you can see who has and has not submitted recommendations through your application portal. Also follow up with a thank you note letting them know where you got in and where you decided to go. They put in effort to help with your application; recognize their efforts.

11. Concluding Thoughts

Recommendation letters can be a very important part of your application and represent one of the few areas of your application that is completely dependent on other people. Make sure you do not wait until the last minute. Try to get some at the end of junior year while you are still fresh in the mind of your teachers. Also, remember you apply at beginning of senior year, so your teachers at that time might not know you as well as some of your junior year teachers. Pick a variety of recommenders and ask for more than you need just in case.

.

11. Action items

- ❏ Make a list of potential recommenders and be purposeful with who you ask
- ❏ Decide what you would like them to say about you
- ❏ Write individualized letters to request each recommendation
- ❏ Hand deliver a request letter and resume whenever possible
- ❏ Make an impression on all your teachers, advisors, bosses, and other adults in your life by being positive, inquisitive, and helpful

Chapter 12:

The interview

12.1 Nail your interview

The interview is another opportunity to showcase what makes you an ideal candidate for your school of choice. In simple terms, you are hoping that the interview allows you to develop a connection with a representative from your target school who will then go on to advocate for your admission. Many schools say that an interview can only work in your favor, but remember that if it doesn't go in your favor then it has essentially gone against you. This can be a nerve wracking experience for many students, but it should be viewed as an opportunity and not as a roadblock. As with anything, if you are prepared for the interview and have a game plan to follow, then you will be successful in this part of the process. Interviews can happen in person or via Skype or even with a good old fashioned phone call. In each situation the core of what you try to accomplish will remain the same, but how you execute that plan may need to be modified.

Since the interview is all about developing a rapport by speaking with someone, you want to develop this (sometimes lost) skill. You need to get out there and speak to people, preferably people who you don't know very well (obviously be smart about this) and especially adults. Try going into a coffee shop and striking up a conversation with someone, practice on your parents' friends, your friends' parents, and really anyone else who will give you a chance to get a word in. Doing this just once won't help; make it a habit as you prepare for the interview.

12.2 Preparing for the interview

No preparation is never the best option in this scenario. It doesn't matter how skilled you are in the art of small talk; you will need to prepare for this. There are some simple steps to take to make sure that you are ready.

1. **Know your school**: You are applying there so you hopefully know a little about it, but this is the time to become an expert. You should understand the unique cultures and traditions, scheduling requirements, specific programs you want to study, and anything else that you can.
2. **Know your audience**: Once you schedule the interview, familiarize yourself with the person who will be interviewing you. Search for similarities you could have and try to bring those out in your interview. (Of course, do so without seeming like a crazy stalker; never say "I saw on your Facebook profile that you like…").
3. **Know yourself:** Remember to reread your application and the highlights of your resume so you don't leave out any important stories about yourself. In all likelihood your interviewer has not read your application or essays, so you need to convey what you can.
4. **Practice common interview questions aloud**: Use the table below to start to organize your thoughts. This is not something you want to rely on writing out, you want to practice aloud. Time yourself, record yourself, listen to how the answers sound as you speak them.

Commonly Asked Interview Questions

Tell me about yourself.
What makes you a good fit for _____ University? Why should we pick you instead of another applicant?
Where do you see yourself in 5 years? 10 years?
What is the most significant challenge that we face today?
Tell me about a time that you failed and what you learned from the experience.
Recommend a book you have read to me.
Tell me about your favorite class or professor and what you liked about it.

What is your greatest strength? Your greatest weakness?

Tell me about an activity that you participate in and why you like it.

If you had a gap year before college what would you do with it?

Do you have any questions you want to ask me?

Was there anything that you wanted to share with me that you have not had a chance to yet?

It is a good idea to know what is going on in the world before doing an interview in case that comes up. And again, really make sure that you know the school you are interviewing for, inside and out.

12.3 What should you bring with you to the interview

In the interview you hope to become memorable. We suggest bringing two things with you to the interview:

1. Bring your **resume**. You want to be able to hand that to your interviewer right at the start to focus the interview on your best qualities and try to give them some material to ask about.

2. Bring an **artifact**. Bring an item with you that will be memorable and immediately get the interviewer to ask about something you can answer. Have a medal from science fair? Wear it in. Have a picture of your dog you saved from a shelter? Bring it.

Once, during an interview Josh was conducting, a student unrolled a blueprint of her home town on the table in the coffee shop where they were meeting. She brought it to the interview to show him the layout of a city-wide recycling program she had initiated. That was memorable! In addition, consider bringing copies of your application essays in case the interviewer wants to see them.

12.4 Dos and Don'ts

Interviews in general can be intimidating and college interviews can be even more so. If you haven't had many, you need to prepare even more. The good news is there are a lot of things you can do to be ready. Think of your interview like going on a first date. You want to make a good impression. There are simple things that you can do to make the interview work in your favor.

Do...

Be on time: Being late to an interview just should not happen. Leave early- very early if necessary to be sure you arrive on time. If something out of your control should cause you to be late, call your interviewer and let them know.

Be prepared with knowledge about the school: The best way to do this is to have already done a college visit. Other things you can do: go to the website of the department of your intended major and look up some of the professors or look up internship opportunities there. Ideally, not only will you know about the school, but you will have specific questions for the interviewer about their school.

Be enthusiastic about your interest in the school: You want to go to this school- let the interviewer know that. Don't act desperate, but you should always act as if the school you are interviewing for is your top choice.

Dress professionally: Don't dress like you are meeting your friends; dress to impress within reason. When you put on your best clothes you send the signal that you are doing something that is important to you. You can add a little bit of flare if that is your thing, but don't go overboard. This is a professional interview and you need to treat it that way. In order to do that properly, you have to look the part.

Handwrite a thank you note: Writing a thank you note to your interviewer following the interview might seem insignificant, but remember that you are trying to make a connection with someone. If you have received an interview you have already cleared one hurdle. You're in the second round of cuts. A recommendation from your interviewer is key to receiving your acceptance from your desired college.

Bring a polished resume: Someone once said, "Never underestimate the importance of a resume." This is no exception. Bring one with you to hand to the interviewer. Bring a nice one, one that is better than the downloaded and printed copy they have (or don't have for that matter). We are not saying to print it on pink scented paper or anything, but make sure it is high quality. Again, your resume contains all that you want them to know about you, so be prepared to discuss its contents.

Don't...

Be unprepared: One way to make sure you are prepared is to make a list of questions for the interviewer. At some point in every interview, the interviewer will ask, "Do you have any questions for me?" That is your opportunity to turn the interview around and show that you have a real interest in that school specifically. Be prepared to answer the question, "What did you want to tell me that I didn't ask yet?" (the answer is **not,** "We pretty much covered everything").

Be arrogant or off-putting: Being confident in yourself is not the same as being cocky or acting like the interview is just a formality. It is possible to be confident yet humble and appreciative at the same time. If you are well prepared, dress appropriately, speak appropriately, and use good body language and eye contact, you will appear confident. If you show up looking sloppy, use overly familiar or casual language, slouch down into your chair, and don't look like you want to be there, you will not make a good impression.

Make other options seem better: No matter what school you are interviewing for, that school is your number one choice. You're not interested in possibly going there if you don't get into your number one choice, you want to go there exclusively, end of story.

Interview content organizer

What you want them to know about you?	Questions for the interviewer	Why this school? What do you like about the school?

12.5 After the interview

The interview is over, whether you nailed it or just did "ok," what you do next can still have an impact. You want to reaffirm your interest in the college and also solidify yourself as desirable candidate for admission. The easiest way to accomplish these aims is to do it the old fashioned way. Send a heartfelt thank you note. In the day of social media and electronic communications where you may have set up your interview via text, the temptation to just text a quick thank you is understandable. You should do that. But also handwrite a thank you card to send to your interviewer (immediately, since they may submit their official interview report soon after your interview) and remind them once again about how much you want to attend their college and why. Touch on a salient occasion from the interview where you connected and of course sincerely thank them for taking their time to meet with you.

12. Concluding thoughts

Interviews are intimidating to begin with; don't make it worse by showing up unprepared. Keep in mind that, in general, the interviewer is on your side and rooting for you. They want to find someone who is going to impress them and make them excited to recommend. They are hoping that person is you.

This is not something that every applicant gets to do. You have already done enough to get this far. Your goal is to have a great conversation with the interviewer that centers around your goals, who you are as a person, and desire to attend that school. Be prepared for it to be long. In fact, the longer the interview takes, the better. A good interview will last at least an hour. If you are out of there in 30 minutes or less, I hate to break it to you, but it did not go well.

12. Action Items

- ❏ Know where you are going so you get there on time. Drive there before the interview so you are familiar with the route
- ❏ BE ON TIME
- ❏ Make a list of questions you have about the university and for the interviewer
- ❏ Bring an updated copy your resume
- ❏ Every school you interview for is your No. 1 choice…..as far as they know
- ❏ Use appropriate language and dress to impress
- ❏ Buy some thank you cards
- ❏ Record yourself answering interview questions, then watch it
- ❏ Participate in mock interviews

Chapter 13:

After you submit your apps

13.1 After you submit your apps

Kicking apps takes a lot of energy, and it is tempting to kick back and relax once you click submit. Unfortunately, you don't have much time to bask in your accomplishments because your work is far from complete. First, you need to continue to work hard in school and everything else you do. There is a real possibility that you will need to send your college more information about what you have continued to do during senior year, so you cannot just shut it down. The submitted application should not be your final contact with your colleges. You are responsible for advocating for your admission to these colleges, and the application is not the end of that process.

13.2 Confirmation of receipt

Once you submit your app, you assume that everything has been received by your school, but has it? Some items, like your official SAT®/ACT® score reports, and transcripts will be sent separately. Your recommenders upload separately in some cases as well. Do not assume that your colleges received everything. Contact them to confirm that they did receive every part of your application and then be sure to complete the app if anything is missing. This, once again, speaks to the importance of you applying before the actual deadline, so if anything is missing you can be sure that it gets in on time.

13.3 Care packages

Sending a care package about two weeks after you submit your app is a great idea. First, you need to determine if your school will accept it or not. While this may not be explicitly stated, some of the larger state schools will say specifically that they **do not** want any extra materials sent. In these cases, if you send a care package it may actually detract from your application chances. But if the college isn't against receiving supplemental material, then it would be wise to send it. In the worst case scenario, it will not add to your candidacy; in the best case, it will help them get an even more complete picture of you. If you do decide to send a care package, there are a few ground rules:

1. Send it FedEx or another method that requires someone to physically sign to receive it.
2. Address it to a specific person. Do not send it to admissions in general; send it to the specific admissions counselor who is responsible for your region of the country/state.
3. Be thoughtful about what you include. Make it organized and user-friendly; a loose jumble of junk will certainly not help your case.
4. Send it in a timely fashion. If you send it too soon, they may not have even processed your app, too late and the decision may have already been made.
5. If you are sending packages to different schools, be sure to individualize them.

The first item in your care package should be a well-crafted cover letter. The items you include after that may require additional letters that identify or explain them. For example, if you include a picture of you with a child you befriended from the orphanage in Nicaragua that you volunteered at each summer, you need to explain that context to the viewer. Remember the goal is to give depth to your story and your character in ways that the essays and the rest of the written app could not. Some items to consider including are listed below.

If you are planning to include supplemental recommendation letters here, look to expand the pool of recommenders. These are effective if they speak to other aspects of your character and performance in other facets of your life. If you are an athlete get a coach's rec, if you volunteer extensively get you volunteer coordinator's rec, if you are heavily involved with your church or youth group get your pastor's rec, if you do research get you lab supervisor's rec. One recommendation that can be especially effective is the letter from an important alumnus of the college. Any letters included should be signed and sealed before inclusion in the care package.

Care Package contents checklist

List the schools you will send the package to here and cross them off once you mail it to each.	
Item	Included
Cover letter	
Supplemental sealed recommendation letters	
Newspaper clippings	
Copy of awards	
Relevant photos	
Notable Research Papers- senior thesis, IB extended essay, Science Fair project	
Personal artwork	
Multimedia samples	
Hard copy of your resume if it wasn't uploaded	
Extra essays written for other schools that are outstanding	
Other:	
Other:	

A brief word on including multimedia supplemental material: If you are a performer, then a CD with a video of your performance would be great to include. An artist who cannot send actual samples could give a digital tour of various pieces. An athlete can include a highlight film even if they aren't destined to play sports at their college of choice. Again, if it would deepen their understanding of who you are, include it.

There are ways to include this as a more formal part of your app. One is to use a site like www.Zeemee.com which allows you to create a digital portfolio to engage with your admissions counselors. You can do this in a similar way with effective use of social media like creating your own youtube® channel as your showcase.

13.4 Follow up campus visits

If you have not done a formal campus tour yet, then now is the time to do it. Sometimes taking the tour is another mark in your favor because when the college accepts you they know that you have been on campus and know what you are getting into. In addition, some colleges may have more selective visit programs for specific majors, for athletic recruiting, and even for scholarships. Find out if your school has any special visit options and take advantage to let them know that you really are serious about your application.

13.5 Updates

As you continue through senior year and pile on the accolades, it is a good idea to send an update email or two. Unnecessary emails are just an annoyance, but updates with significant content will bring your name back into the consciousness of the admissions staff and maybe prompt them to give your app another look.

13. Concluding Thoughts

Once you submit the applications to your target colleges, your application process is not complete. Make sure you follow up in effective ways to convince them that you are really interested in attending their college. The worst thing that can happen with follow ups is that they fall upon deaf ears and have not added to your candidacy. But what if it can help? Just the effort to follow up says something about you as a potential student and about your desire to attend their school. This could be the X factor that puts you over the top. Why not try it?

13. Action Items

- ❏ Confirm that your application is complete once you submit it
- ❏ Follow up with a care package sent to those colleges that will accept it. Include items that will make your application more compelling and more complete
- ❏ Follow up with your colleges once or twice later on in the decision process just to keep your name on their radar

Chapter 14:

Decision time

14.1 Acceptance and Rejection

The simplest way that this journey ends for students is acceptance to an early decision school in December. No choices to make, nothing to wait on. Most students aren't that lucky, though, and there will be some tough decisions to make. The critical part of this is to stay engaged with your academics and activities and continue to make progress.

14.2 Making your decision

You applied to multiple schools at the start of the process and now you have heard back from them. You won some, you lost some- but in the end you were accepted to multiple schools. Now it is decision time! So how do you decide? There are a number of factors that will influence this decision since you did your homework and all of your schools you applied to would be a great fit for you. So how do you decide? The questions below are designed to help you with this process:

1. When you initially selected schools you ranked them. Look back to your table in chapter 6 and start there. Is there any reason that your ranking is now different?

2. Which of your colleges will prepare you best of your intended career? Look even deeper now at course offerings, program requirements, study abroad opportunities, campus resources, etc.

3. What are the employment resources and networking opportunities that will be available to you when you graduate?

4. What resources and support will be available to you when you begin your journey at each school (advisement, social support, etc.)? Do those resources expand and continue through your years on campus?

5. What are the differences in financial aid offered by each college? It may be worth revisiting ROI calculators as you see what the cost will get you in return.

6. Which one *feels* right?

7. How hard are you wanting/willing to work? At this stage some students reassess and bow out of ultra-competitive schools even if they have been admitted.

It should go without saying, but make sure that you visit the schools you are deciding between (and maybe even visit them again if you already have). You will be surprised how your perspective can change by this point in the process and another visit can help you clarify your feelings further. In the end, a good old fashioned list of pros and cons of your different schools can help as well. Use the table below and fill it in over a series of days to help you get an unbiased, well-thought-out selection of options. You shouldn't really need to compare more than four colleges in this way, but if you do as always you can find more tables under our app kicking resources at www.kickingapps.org

College Choice Matrix

College:		College:	
Pros	Cons	Pros	Cons

College:		College:	
Pros	Cons	Pros	Cons

14.3 Deferral

If you applied early then the best outcome is acceptance, the worst is rejection, and the limbo state between them is deferral. In simple terms, deferral means that the college is interested in you but not totally sold. They want to give your application more consideration after they see the rest of the regular decision class. The key with deferral is to remember two things:

1. Your admission is not certain, so finish up all of your other apps and submit them.
2. You need to be actively involved in the deferral process. You now have another opportunity to convince them to admit you. Use it.

The first thing you can do is to make sure that now (and really throughout senior year) you keep doing everything you always did and then more. You want to show the admissions officers that you continue to be an active and involved member of your high school community. You need to keep doing this so that you have items to brag about in your deferral response letter as well. In general, this letter is broken into three parts and you can see an example below.

Deferral Response format

1. Introduction: Introduce yourself and thank them for considering your application.

2. Body: Update them on all the great things you have done since you submitted your initial application.

3. Conclusion: Reaffirm your commitment their college and your connection to what they are all about.

Example deferral response letter JA- accepted regular decision Dartmouth

Dear Dean XXX,

Thank you for considering my application for early admission to the Dartmouth class of 2019. I applied early because I am committed to attending Dartmouth, and your decision only intensifies that desire. Although I am disappointed by my deferral from the Early Decision pool, I am continuing to set my sights on Dartmouth for my college career.

Since my initial application I have continued to follow a rigorous program of studies in my senior year. According to my father's explanation of the learning pyramid, I am adding depth to my understanding of both Calculus and Physics by tutoring other students weekly. My senior classes include five Advanced Placement classes with a midterm weighted GPA of 4.86. My work with the Starkey Foundation to provide hearing aids to the underserved has continued and I have provided an outreach to the Easter Seals organization to incorporate pediatric hearing aids into this charity work

I know that Dartmouth offers the best undergraduate education in the United States and I wish to become a part of that program and add to it. Throughout my life I have encountered many obstacles due to my extensive hearing disability. I see this deferral as yet another hurdle to overcome and hope that as you reconsider my application you will be reminded of the grit and determination that have carried me this far. I am hopeful and optimistic that you will consider me for admission to Dartmouth so that I can further my studies in Physics as I work toward a career in medicine.

Sincerely,

JA

One good spin on this is to send a postcard. Certainly some people will send nothing, but most people who really want to get into a school will send something. So how about making this personal and memorable? You could make a postcard pretty easily with any given online print or photo site. Make sure that the image and content are memorable.

Some schools, like Stanford for example, have a specific form that they want deferred students to fill out. Make sure to check to see if your college has a specific form and if they do, put your heart and soul into filling it out.

14.4 The dreaded waitlist

Regular decision has its own version of deferral: the waitlist. This outcome parallels the deferral in many ways. Again, the school is interested in you, but just not as interested as they are in all of the other students who they admitted immediately. Schools always admit more students than they think will attend. If there is still space in their incoming class after they offer admission to everyone, then they will extend invitations to students on the waitlist. The difference with the waitlist is that you will actually need to accept the offer of admission from another college and pay your deposit and all the rest while still remaining on the waitlist. You may actually not get an offer of admission until the summer or later, so be ready with your decision should it come.

Your responsibilities on the waitlist are the same as they would be if you were deferred. There is usually a specific form to fill out to stay on the list. Then follow it with a letter or postcard styled after the example above in the deferral section. One of the best strategies for the students on the waitlist is to do another formal visit. Reaffirming your commitment to attend the school will set you apart from other waitlist candidates.

14.5 Rejection and dealing with it

Rejection is part of life and in the maturation process that hopefully comes with the college search. Application rejection will be something most of you experience. How you deal with rejection says a lot about your character. If you are rejected, be sad about it, face the emotions that it causes within you, but then take a deep breath and move forward. Reflect. Think about why you were rejected, what you could have done differently, then, act on that. Rejection is an opportunity for growth and self-improvement. Take advantage of it and be better. We also always recommend that you save all of your rejections, in hard copy, and then use them for motivation in the future. Work to prove that the people who rejected you were wrong.

14. Concluding Thoughts

When you hear back from a college, the decision that you have been anticipating for months finally arrives. Hopefully it is an acceptance, but sometimes it is not. Remember that sometimes this outcome is less about you and more about them. Maybe in this particular year your doppelganger also applied but they had 10 points more on the SAT® or a funnier essay. If you were accepted, then you need to make final decisions about where you will attend and if you were rejected, you need to determine your alternative course of action. Remember to do everything else that you need to at the end of senior year- including finishing strong on your academics and final standardized tests- to make sure that you solidify the name you have worked so hard to make throughout the process.

14. Action Items

- ❏ Carefully consider your admissions offers and pick the one that is BEST FOR YOU
- ❏ If you are deferred, actively respond to the college and fight for admission
- ❏ If you are waitlisted, decide if you want a spot on the waitlist, accept an offer from another school you want, and then fight for admission off the waitlist
- ❏ Embrace rejection as an opportunity to reflect and grow

Chapter 15:

Finishing Strong

15.1 I'm going to college next year. Now what?

So **you kicked apps, you made a name for yourself** and you were successful in the application process. You were admitted to multiple schools and after weighing your options you made the best choice for you and your future. You submitted the deposit and then you paused for a moment to catch your breath. As with anything done well, you are not really done. Time to tie up some loose ends and make sure you are ready for the fall.

15.2 Finish senior year strong

The proverbial senior slide is always a temptation at this point. You have worked so hard for so long, so why not just hit cruise control and have fun? After all, you have accomplished what you set out to do. While this temptation is understandable, you need to avoid succumbing to it. You have worked too hard to let it slip away. Consider the following points:

1. Remember that colleges can always rescind your offer of admission. If you take a nosedive, you might get a letter- and if it is serious enough you might find yourself no longer invited to the party.

2. Your end-of-the-year exams for AP, AICE, and IB still matter. Whether it is for college credit or college placement, these scores will affect you for years to come. In addition, an AICE or IB diploma can have other benefits, including scholarship money at some colleges.

3. Continuing to develop good study habits and retaining more information will be helpful as you move on to the next level in college.

4. Your final standing and GPA may be helpful in getting you into lab positions, leadership positions, and even specific classes early in your college career.

15.3 Paying for College

Scholarships

Finding scholarships can be a frustrating process. You constantly hear about how much money in scholarships goes unclaimed every year, so where is the money? The key to getting scholarships is to apply to as many as you can. The rule of thumb in the financial aid world is fifteen to one. For every 15 scholarship applications you fill out, you'll get one. It is a volume activity. So where do you look?

Your high school: Start with your school counselor. Most schools maintain some database or website of local scholarships. Apply to any and all local scholarships that you even remotely qualify for. Don't disqualify yourself before they do.

Other high schools in your area (especially public schools): Check other school websites for local scholarships in their area. Remember that this is a numbers game, so even if you only find one $500 scholarship, that is $500 less out of your pocket.

Student jobs: If you have a part-time job with a major retailer, fast food chain, or grocery store, there may be a scholarship you can apply for through the human resources department. Some companies offer tuition reimbursement for classes. These are often easier to get, and although it is not up-front money, every bit helps.

Parent jobs: Likewise, scholarships and tuition assistance programs could be available for students through their parents' employers.

Scholarship search engines: There are a number of free scholarship sites that match you up with available scholarships. As a general rule, you should not have to pay to get scholarships. Fastweb.com and scholarships.com are two commonly used search engines. You create a profile and receive a list of the scholarships that you could qualify for. The key to success is to make sure your profile casts a wide enough net, and again apply to every single one that you can.

Micro-scholarships: This is relatively new form of scholarship that can be somewhat deceiving at first. Rasie.me is an example of this type of site. These scholarships work by qualifying you for university-based money for the classes and activities you do. For example, you get $100 for taking an AP class. This only works for schools that are a member of the site, and it does not stack. This type of site pre-qualifies you for school-based money, meaning that if you qualify for $25,000 to attend a school, that is the least amount of money that the school will offer you, and they may even offer you more. They will not, however, offer you $30,000 and then add on the $25,000 from your GoFundMe account. Even though it is not additional money, it is still worth doing especially if you start during your freshmen year in high school.

Philanthropic Organizations: There are innumerable social clubs, community organizations, and nonprofits out there. These are often the scholarships that go unclaimed every year. You don't have to be member or related to member; you just have to find out about it and apply. Researching these type of organizations in your area would be great to do during junior year. Even though you may not be able to apply as a junior, these scholarships are often offered every year. Generally speaking, scholarship applications don't change much from year to year, so you would have a jump on everyone else. Some places to consider: Rotary Club, the Elks Lodge, Freemasons, YMCA, Churches, Lions Club, your local Chamber of Commerce. This is another area where you school counselor can help out. These organizations often approach schools looking for students to award these scholarships to. So make sure someone will give out your name when the time comes.

Federal grants and loans

For the majority of you, filling out the Free Application for Federal Student Aid (FASFA) will be your first step in the financial aid process. Notice the first word is free. If you end up on a site trying to charge you a fee for to apply for federal student aid, you are in the wrong place. This is a two-part online application that requires reporting of both the parents' and student's income. Based on your demographics, income, and assets, you may qualify for federal grants (which do not need to be paid back) or loans (which do need to be paid back).

There are a few issues to consider before accepting loans. First, the loans belong to the student. The parent may be asked to cosign the loan, but the debt belongs to the student and must be repaid beginning within six months of completing college. Second, because of this fact, may people are scared of student loans. True, you want to avoid them if possible, but, like credit cards, they have a place and a purpose and, when used correctly, can be a good option. Your ideal situation would be to not take any loans if possible, but if you need to use loans, just be responsible about them.

CSS Profile

The CSS profile is used by some colleges and scholarship programs to qualify students for non-federal financial aid. This is used in addition to the FAFSA, not in substitution for it. The FAFSA qualifies you for Federal Grants; the CSS Profile qualifies you for institutional non-federal financial aid. There is a Fee of $25 to complete the profile and then a fee for each college or scholarship you submit the profile to. The College Board (yes, the same company that brought you hits such as the SAT®, AP, and SAT 2 Subject Exams) does offer a fee waiver based on financial need.

15.4 Use the summer to get a head start

The summer after your senior year is a great time to get a head start on your college course work. Some colleges offer and even encourage a shortened summer term for students to get on campus and acclimate to the environment and the course work. Even if you don't go to your college, you might consider taking or even auditing a few college classes at the local community college to brush up on some rusty areas or get a head start on content you know you will face. If you want to go pre-med and know that first semester you will get crushed with Calculus and General Chemistry and all the rest, why not brush up on your Calculus over the summer so the fall, at least in that class, will be a breeze?

15.5 Get some Experience

If you know you are going into a particular field, then getting more experience in that field this summer will help. You will not only be adding to the skill set you need to develop, but you will also continue to build your resume. If you are planning to study science, then doing some research over the summer would be a great way to build your skills and make connections. Planning on going into law? How about working at a local law firm? Want to be a teacher? Take the opportunity this summer to work with kids, be a camp counselor, or work for a tutoring center.

15.6 Broaden your worldview

This summer can also present you with the opportunity to expand your worldview through travel and volunteerism. As you move into college, one of the soft skills you will develop is a greater degree of introspection. To be able to do this effectively requires that you have more experience under your belt. Giving back to your community or to underprivileged people around the world can help to accomplish this aim. Travel can do the same. We aren't really advocating for the grad trip to Cancun, but real experiential travel that can open your eyes to other customs, traditions and natural places around the world, can do a lot to recharge your batteries and get you ready for the broader cultural immersion you will experience in college.

15. Concluding thoughts

Once you are accepted into college, you can catch your breath but your work isn't done. Be sure that you finish strong academically and make the most of your remaining time in high school. Do not blow off your exams senior spring- there is a lot riding on them. Much of the time during senior year and after your acceptance should be spent finding scholarships. Apply to as many as possible, and remember that your intended major does not have to be what you actually end up majoring in. It is time consuming, yes, but your senior year will come and go, while college debt is forever (or at least seems like it while you are trying to pay it off). Get out into your community and start looking for which organizations give out scholarships, and talk to current seniors or recent graduates to find out about unknown scholarships. No amount is too small to be worth applying for. Then, when the work is done and senior year is over, make your summer count.

15. Action Items

- ❏ Finish senior year strong
- ❏ Sign up for a scholarship search engine
- ❏ Meet with your counselor to find out about your school's scholarship resources
- ❏ Look for philanthropic organizations in your community
- ❏ Ask current seniors and recent graduates about scholarships they applied for
- ❏ Sign up for a micro-scholarship site
- ❏ Apply to as many scholarships as you can. Remember the 15 to 1 ratio
- ❏ Make plans for senior summer that will benefit you in the coming years

Chapter 16:

Kicking Apps and Making Names

16.1 Concluding Thoughts

Now What?

If you have reached the end of the guide and you have not completed the college application process, now is the time to prioritize the contents of the preceding chapters and begin to make your name and get ready to kick apps. Start with a simple to do list and then work to accomplish those items, then check them off as you go

To Do

Action	Resources needed/concerns	Complete

If you have completed the application process then it is time to think about the next steps as you move ahead into college.

Support on your Journey

While no single resource can encapsulate the entire application process, we hope that this guide has helped you to **kick apps and make a name for yourself**. If you need to go deeper or need more direct assistance with the process, we are here to help. We work with hundreds of students each year from all around the country in various aspects of the application process. Sometimes a guiding hand, an experienced set of eyes, or even just a calming influence can make the difference between admission to your target school and the alternative. Contact us today to set up a consultation at 386-405-2128

The Big Picture

In moments of frustration when you are feeling especially overwhelmed by the scope of this process it helps to take a step back and consider the big picture Always remember that you are participating in a self-development process. Either you are setting out to forge a path of self-growth, or you are reflecting back on the events and relationships that have shaped who you are today. Regardless of where you are on this journey, this book is intended to guide you through creating a complete, accurate, and engaging picture of yourself.

Kicking apps and making names is not accomplished overnight, so be cautious of any program, person or company who claims to be able to do just that for you. There are some who offer to write your essay or give you the perfect topic. Be skeptical of programs that guarantee to get you admitted into medical school or Harvard Law.

The most valuable experiences are those that challenge or inspire you. If what you are considering doesn't do either or both of those things, then not only will it not add your application, but it is probably not worth doing at all. If your primary goal is to learn about yourself, your strengths, and your passions then you will not only **Kick Apps**, but you may even find your broader life's purpose in the process.

Want more personal help Kicking Apps? Need guidance about how to Make your Name?

Platt and Chiofalo are available to help.

Contact us today:

www.kickingapps.org

kickingappsmakingnames@gmail.com

386-405-2128

Individual Assistance

Comprehensive College Consulting · Essay review

Resume development · Project design · Mentorship

Large Group programs available as well

One day college application workshops · Week long bootcamps

Staff professional development · Motivational speaking

About the Authors

Joshua Platt is the founder and lead college consultant at Ace It Test Prep, LLC. For over a decade, he has run this boutique test prep and college consulting company in east central Florida, helping students from across the southeastern United States navigate the college application landscape. A self-proclaimed idealist, his focus is always to guide students through the college process by fostering their personal growth and maturation along the way. His former clients attend prestigious colleges around the country. A graduate of Dartmouth College himself and now an alumni interviewer for the college, Joshua has a personal understanding of the complexity of the application process in general as well as the specific requirements for admissions to elite colleges.

A veteran teacher with 19 years of classroom experience he is passionate about science, teaching AP and IB Environmental Science and IB Biology. A winner of Teacher of the Year honors at two different schools and a National Board Certified teacher, Joshua is a proponent of education and views college as the gateway to success for most students. He also works for the IBO serving as a workshop leader and a site visitor for the organization.

Joshua is a Boston native and die-hard Red Sox fan. He currently resides in Florida with his wife Lauren and sons Jordan and Colin. He credits Lauren, Jordan and Colin for providing him with daily inspiration to pursue a career in education and help students to achieve their dreams.

Jacob Chiofalo is a high school counselor and a private college consultant. Jacob has helped students and parents from a variety of backgrounds gain admission to their dream colleges, universities, and academies. He has worked in a variety of settings including, private, public, and international schools. Jacob has helped literally hundreds of students and parents through the entire process described in this book, from class selection, to career exploration, and finally to college selection and application completion.

Having worked internationally and seeing the importance of the role of education in society, Jacob is an ardent supporter of public education and the value that an advanced education can provide. This belief is what has inspired him to participate in writing this book. The impact the right choices can make on a young person's life is much too big to be left to chance.

Originally from a small town in Long Island NY, Jacob has lived and worked in Florida for the last 6 years with his wife Shannon, his two kids Lily and Jacob, and his dog Peacey (named by Lily when she was 4 years old) who are all NY Giants fans.

Acknowledgements

A special thank you to Lauren, for your love and support throughout the writing of this book and the challenges of starting and running this small business. You are my rock and my world and I am so fortunate to have you in my life each day. Thank you Jordan and Colin for motivating me to be the best I can be every day. Your energy and enthusiasm for life inspires me to tirelessly approach each day.

I would like to thank my wife Shannon for always supporting me and pushing me to be my best. To my daughter Lily who continues to amaze me every day with her beautifully unique way of seeing the world and to my son Jacob who makes me laugh every day and is possibly the coolest kid ever. You all are my whole reason for everything I do. Thank you.

Special thanks to Robbie Harms for all your help in the editing and completion of this book.

Made in United States
North Haven, CT
06 June 2022

19901449R00096